The Porsche 911

Patrick Paternie

MBI Publishing Company

This edition published in 2003 by MBI Publishing Company, Galtier Plaza, Suite 200, 380 Jackson Street, St. Paul, MN 55101-3885 USA

MBI Publishing Company books are also available at discounts in bulk quantity for industrial or sales-promotional use. For details write to Special Sales Manager at Motorbooks International Wholesalers & Distributors, Galtier Plaza, Suite 200, 380 Jackson Street, St. Paul, MN 55101-3885 USA.

ISBN 0-7603-1699-6

Printed in China

CONTENTS

ACKNOWLEDGMENTS

First off, I need to thank the usual suspects for their patience and support during the "birthing process" of this book. Unfortunately, unlike mothers delivering real babies into this world, my moaning, whining, or whimpering is stretched out over the entire period of gestation. So hats off to my wife, Linda, my kids, friends, and associates for bearing with me.

My editor, John Adams-Graf of MBI Publishing Company, not only puts up with my whining and excuses but probably thinks up even better ones for me to stay in good graces with our collective boss at MBI, Zack Miller. John is also a hardcore 911 enthusiast, so he serves as good inspiration as well.

I can always count on Matt Stone for whatever I may need at any given time. And of course my "sponsor" who helped me tumble down the rabbit hole into the crazy world of automotive writing, the infamous Larry B., wherever he is today.

It is also an honor and a pleasure to have the photographic excellence of Randy Leffingwell and Les Bidrawn to accompany my words.

Thanks to all the wonderful people and places that you discover just hanging around Porsche 911s. People who lent their time and in many cases their cars so this book could come together include Bruce Sansone, Jim Edwards, Pete Lech, Richard Price, Gary Barnhill, Stewart Thomas, Hal Holleman, Randy Garell, and Ed Buliavac. Ted Mumm, Cris Huergas, Phil and Pat Van Buskirk, and Craig Stevenson also made contributions that are appreciated.

I am also grateful to Jens Torner at Porsche AG, who has always been generous with factory photos and information whenever I contact him. The same is true for Bob Carlson and Eleanor Smith at Porsche Cars North America.

Cris Huergas, Freeman Thomas, Kevin Beard, Pete Johnson, and all the others who make up the R Gruppe get a special thanks for being the quintessential 911 enthusiasts. They are "keepers of the flame" dedicated to keeping the original sports car concept of the 911 alive. Their old hot rod 911s are done the way that would make both Steve McQueen and Michael Delaney break into that little smirk and present a raised thumb salute.

INTRODUCTION

For the best introduction as to what it is about the 911 that transforms its drivers into enthusiasts, I must defer to Steve McQueen who captured the essence of the 911 in the opening scenes for his movie Le Mans. The racing film, which probably has the least human dialogue since 'talkies' were invented, lets a slate gray 911S coupe do the talking as the camera follows its classic silhouette through the French countryside to the town of Le Mans and then out on the 24 Hour race circuit. (I know it looks black, but you can't be a true Porschephile unless you study up on arcane details like this.) The only sound is the unique whirring, metallic cacophony of the air-cooled 911 flat six-cylinder as McQueen's character, Michael Delaney, puts it through its paces.

(More trivia: Delaney, in a later scene on one of the rare occasions he does speak, utters the immortal phrase: "Racing is life. Anything that happens before or after is just waiting." Owners of 911s can relate to this thinking in terms of time spent behind the wheel of other cars.)

Porsche, with 16 overall victories, is synonymous with Le Mans. And a big part of the spell cast by the 911 is that when your left hand twists the ignition key, no matter how mundane your actual commute, you feel like Michael Delaney at Le Mans. The view through the panoramic arch of the windshield, over the wipers parked at its base, and between the front fenders at the road disappearing under the sloping hood, even at 20 miles per hour, evokes fantasies of being in the cockpit of a legendary Porsche 917 as it gobbles up the tarmac of the Mulsanne Straight. Look down at the dashboard and, as in a race car, a big round tachometer stares back, the speedometer relegated to the side. The tach's needle acts as a baton leading a concert of raucous sounds from the rear that covers a scale from muted whine to guttural moan to high-pitched snarl. A breathtaking experience, or as in the case of Michael Delaney, one that leaves you speechless.

What other car approaches the level at which the 911 combines the sounds and sensations of a race car in a package that can be reasonably driven to work every day? In fact, until recently, when the firm's lawyers and accountants became as important as its engineers, Porsche prided itself in offering 911 models that could be driven directly to the racetrack from the showroom floor.

Another part of the 911 mystique is that, for most of its life, with one swift twitch of its engine-laden tail, it could separate the enthusiasts from the dilettantes and poseurs, usually by tossing the latter off into the trees. Once again, it's that race car attitude in a world where "user friendly" equates to the lowest common denominator. Be smooth, pay attention to the feedback through the steering wheel, and be sensitive to how weight transfers while braking, cornering, or accelerating, and driving a 911 is definately an exhilarating experience. Sure the engine is hanging out back, but the driver's butt sits centered between the front and rear wheels. An ideal spot for sensing what the car is doing. Developing a "feel" for what the 911 is communicating takes practice, preferably in a wide open area, but it forms a bond between driver and vehicle that transforms one from an owner to an enthusiast.

Ever the classic, the 911 never forgets its roots yet manages to be a trendsetter as well. Turbochargers, whale tails, biplane wings, and painted brake calipers all debuted on 911s through the years. The 911 was the only sports car to make the top five list of the greatest cars of the twentieth century, which, as Muhammad Ali would say, at this point in history also means for "all time." The 911 is the only car of the five that has continuously remained in production—a side benefit for all of its enthusiastic fans, because that means they can't be accused of being "old car freaks."

So much for the philosophical aspects of the 911's classification as an enthusiast's car. The following chapters will give you a short course in the car's history and development, which, and it should not come as a surprise, was carried out by a dedicated corps of 911 enthusiasts.

Of course, the best introduction to understanding a 911 is by driving one. That's what Michael Delaney would tell you.

The 1967 911S established Porsche as a manufacturer capable of making a world class high-performance GT. Many Porschephiles consider the 1967 911S to be the perfect example of a European version of a "muscle car" that offers quick quarter-mile acceleration times combined with outstanding handling and high top speed. The 1967 911S could deliver 15-second runs at the drag strip and 140 miles per hour on the autobahn. *Les Bidrawn*

THE EVOLUTION BEGINS
BUTZI DRAWS THE LINE

For 36 years and still counting, although the mechanicals underneath have undergone significant changes, the unmistakable profile of the 911 has remained essentially the same. So much so that Porsche has used the 911's outline as a logo. It ranks as one of the most recognizable silhouettes this side of a Coke bottle.

Ferdinand Porsche III, son of Dr. Ferry Porsche and nicknamed "Butzi," is the man responsible for composing this distinctive shape. It evolved from sketches he first drew in August 1959 and altered as the decision process regarding the car's dimensions, seating arrangements, and powertrain continued until 1963.

Butzi's inspiration began by borrowing the high-mounted headlights of the 356. He considered them to be an important part of the "face" that the world recognized as a Porsche. He accentuated them with a lower, flatter trunk lid. From there back he penned the curve that the world then, and well into the future, would recognize as

the 911—a steeply angled windshield topped by a roofline that gracefully spilled rearward down to the taillights and bumpers.

Butzi and his father had begun planning a successor to the 356 as far back as 1956. Remember that Porsche had been founded in 1930 as an engineering consulting firm and not an automobile company. Market demand for what began as a postwar sports car project propelled Porsche into the automobile business and the manufacture of the 356. Like many businesses before and after (Steve Jobs and the Apple computer being a textbook example), the Porsche family's dilemma was what to do for an encore after coming up with such a signature initial product. Ferry Porsche, as an engineer, realized that despite its sales success and loyal following, the 356 was really stretching the limit of engineering work and technology that traced its roots back to the prewar Volkswagen project. More importantly, Ferry Porsche, the marketeer, understood that the problem wasn't

Ferry Porsche and a 1968 911. Porsche passed away in 1998, but the design criteria he established for the successor to the 356 lives on, as the 911 moves into the twenty-first century. What Ferry Porsche decided was that Porsche should stick to what it did best, by making the 911 a bit roomier than the 356 but still a two-seater. He determined that the wheelbase for the new car would be 4.4 inches longer, for a total of 87.0 inches. He also specified that a six-cylinder power plant with overhead camshafts, as opposed to a pushrod-actuated valve train, be used. After he established these initial criteria he handed over the design to his Chief of Styling, and son, Butzi Porsche. *Porsche AG*

simply one of designing a more modern car, it was designing a more modern *Porsche*. The task was to take the sports car prowess melded to the sturdy and practical nature of the 356—what people had come to expect a Porsche to be—and carry it forward in a design that could stay ahead of the ever quickening pace of an automotive world that was approaching full stride as its war wounds healed.

After toying with a number of styling themes and engine combinations, including a full four-seat model, Ferry Porsche laid down two key stipulations that affected the ultimate form of the model that would be known initially as the Porsche 901. The first was that the wheelbase of the new car should be 87 inches, 4.4 inches longer than the 356, primarily to improve the ride. The other decision by Ferry Porsche was that the new car's six-cylinder engine would not have a pushrod-actuated valve train, but a modern overhead camshaft design. A six-cylinder was deemed necessary to keep up with the more powerful offerings of competitors like Jaguar. Company tradition, experience, and knowledge combined with what best fit in the 911's tail section to decide in favor of the engine being air-cooled. A key figure in working out the intricacies of the overhead camshaft valve train for the 901 engine was a young engineer named Ferdinand Piëch. Piëch would continue to play a major role in the development and success of the earlier 911s as well as being the driving force behind Porsche's rise to

Ferdinand Porsche (Butzi), Ferry's son and grandson of company founder Ferdinand Porsche, poses with a 1963 Porsche 901. He was only 28 years old in 1963 when the 911 made its debut. As Chief of Styling, Butzi had the task of designing a car that would link Porsche's past with its future. Today, the familiar profile Butzi created for the 911 is as recognizable as that of a Coca-Cola bottle. Butzi followed up the 911 with another timeless expression of the Porsche essence, the 1964 Porsche 904. *Porsche AG*

dominance in sports car and endurance racing during the late 1960s and 1970s.

The Porsche 911, then known as the 901, made its world debut on September 12, 1963, at the Frankfurt International Auto Show. At least part

Who Are All These Guys Named Ferdinand?

A Quick Climb up the Porsche Family Tree

Professor Ferdinand Porsche, patriarch of the Porsche clan, was born in 1876. In 1930, he founded the eponymous consulting firm that would eventually become one of the world's most respected sports car manufacturers. It was officially registered by the German government in 1931. Among some of Professor Porsche's more notable automotive projects were the Mercedes-Benz SS and SSK supercharger-powered roadsters of the late 1920s, the rear-engined "Silver Arrow" Auto Union race cars of the 1930s, and the first Volkswagen.

Ferdinand Porsche and his wife, Aloisia Kaes, had two children. A daughter, Louise, born in 1904, and a son, Ferdinand Anton Ernst, nicknamed Ferry, who was born in 1909. Louise married Dr. Anton Piëch. Both Piëch and Ferry Porsche went to work in the senior Porsche's consulting firm. Piëch, an attorney, handled contract negotiations, while Ferry Porsche followed in his father's footsteps as a design engineer. Louise also followed in her father's footsteps, with an understanding of the technical aspects as well as a love of automobiles.

Following World War II, Ferdinand Sr., Ferry, and Anton Piëch were imprisoned by the French and for a time Louise Piëch was left to manage the company on her own. Ahead of her time, Louise was a skillful businessperson and an ardent automobile enthusiast, who continued to be involved in company affairs during her lifetime. After an active role as a race driver during the 1930s, in 1949 she began developing the company that would become the successful importer of Volkswagen and Porsche cars to Austria.

Ferry was released in July 1946 but it was a year later, in August 1947, that the elder Porsche and Anton Piëch were finally freed. Professor Ferdinand Porsche died in 1951, and Anton Piëch died of a heart attack the next year.

The next generation of the Porsche family tree entered the business during the 1960s. Ferry and his wife, Dorothea, had four children—Ferdinand III, Wolfgang, Gerd, and Hans-Peter. The eldest son, Ferdinand Porsche III, called Butzi, worked his way up to be the head of the styling department, and left his mark as the designer of both the 904 and the 911. His brother Hans-Peter Porsche joined the company in 1963. Louise Piëch had four children, and three went to work in the company—Michael, Ernst, and Ferdinand. Working in research and development, Ferdinand Piëch played a dynamic role in the development of the 911 and Porsche's racing efforts, before leaving the company in 1972 and ending up at Audi's R&D department. Today he is the chairman of the board of Volkswagen. Butzi also left in 1972 to set up his own firm, Porsche Design, which is best known for its Carrera Design eyewear and line of Porsche watches and chronographs.

The departure of Butzi and Ferdinand Piëch was the fallout from a decision made by Ferry Porsche in 1971 to take the business from a closely held family-run company to a corporate entity. He feared that family squabbles over management would hurt the company, and he encouraged all family members to assume passive roles. The Porsche and Piëch families retained all the shares of Porsche AG until it went public in 1984.

Ferry Porsche died in 1998, and his sister, Louise Piëch, died the following year.

Porsche tried a number of iterations before it decided on the eloquently simple shape of the 911. Best guess is that this split-window Batmobile was an attempt to camouflage the new design for public road testing, and not a desire to make the 911 the Cadillac of sports cars. *Porsche AG*

of it did, as the yellow car on display was a prototype (Chassis 13 325, Number 5 of 13 prototypes produced between 1962 and 1964), with a nonoperational mock-up of the six-cylinder engine in its engine compartment. This car continued to appear at auto shows until February 1964, when it was fitted with a working engine and used on sales tours to dealers throughout

Europe. In December 1965, a testing accident sent the car to the scrap heap, a fate met by all but one of the 13 prototype 901s. Only Number 7, Chassis 13 327, survives in the hands of a private U.S. Porsche collector.

Production of the 911 began a year after its unveiling in September 1964. Considered 1965 models, 235 cars were produced until production

shut down for the holidays in December 1964. Starting up again the following January and continuing through July 1965, Porsche turned out an additional 3,154 of the new 911s to complete the production run for the model year 1965. Subsequent model years all had production terms starting in August and ending the following July.

The first series of 911s are known as the "0" series cars and were made from 1964 to 1967. It was February 1965 when the 911 reached the United States bearing a sticker price of $6,500. A new 1965 356 SC cost $4,577. What you got for the extra two grand was a car that had almost twice the luggage capacity of the 356, a slipperier body (coefficient of drag was 0.380 for the 911 versus the 356's 0.398), and modern, for that time, touches like rack-and-pinion steering, MacPherson strut front suspension, and an independent rear suspension with semitrailing arms instead of archaic swing-axles. The 911 also had a five-speed synchromesh transmission and a 2.0-liter (1,991-cc) overhead cam six-cylinder engine (with a dry sump lubrication system like many race cars) that put out 130 horsepower versus the 356 SC overhead valve four-cylinder's 95 horsepower. Both

Top, left: Porsche was still deciding on final details for the 911 right up to the car's debut. This 1963 photo shows that the twin grilles of the 356 were first considered for the rear deck of the 901. *Porsche AG*

Center: Interim concept for air vent on 901 engine cover depicts an intermediate stage in the evolution of the twin grilles from the 356 coming together in a single vent as the 901 neared its final form in 1963. *Porsche AG*

Bottom: Final iteration of 901 rear deck lid had the air grille spread horizontally across the entire width, in what has become a design characteristic of the 911. *Porsche AG*

Ferry Porsche checks out the latest 1965 911s to roll out of Werk II at Zuffenhausen. Bodies for the 911 were initially supplied by Reutter, which had been building bodies for Porsche since 1951. In 1963, Porsche acquired the Zuffenhausen body plant from the Reutter family when the owners balked at making the investment necessary to begin production of the 911. *Porsche AG*

Go ahead. Drive it. You'll never forget

This 1965 advertisement for the new Porsche stressed the aerodynamic efficiency, added room, and racing-bred development of the 911. Thirty-five years later, Porsche's ad copy for the 911 can boast the same attributes.

the 356 SC and the 911 had four-wheel disc brakes, similar 11.2-inch rear discs, and the 911 had slightly larger-diameter 11.1-inch front discs, versus 10.8-inch on the 356 SC. The two models shared 4.5Jx15-inch steel wheels with 165HRx15 radial tires. The 911 weighed almost 400 pounds more (2,376 pounds versus 1,980 pounds), but its average 0 to 60 time of 8 seconds was about 2.5 seconds quicker, and top speed was 15 miles per hour higher at 130 miles per hour. In 1966, the 912 replaced the 356 SC, mating the 911 body with the SC 1.6-liter four-cylinder engine. At $113 more and 154 pounds heavier, it took 11.7 seconds to go from 0 to 60 miles per hour. Customers didn't seem to miss the 356, because that year Porsche built a record 12,820 cars, of which 9,090 were

912s. About half of the cars produced went to the United States, quickly establishing the popularity of the 900-series cars in this country.

A key ingredient in maintaining the 911's popularity during its long lifespan has been that, starting with the earliest production versions, evolution has been a key part of the manufacturing process. The spin-off of the four-cylinder 912 is an obvious example, but other running changes and design tweaks—from improved external door handles, to changes of the interior trim and storage pockets, to mounting Weber carburetors— were common practice, as the factory approached the 911's early years as a work in progress. Part of the charm of crawling around a 900-series car that has retained its original condition is discovering

Business was booming for Porsche's 900-series cars, thanks to the American market's acceptance of the four-cylinder 912 variant of the 911. This 1967 photo shows production lines building 911s and four-cylinder 912s side-by-side. Production of the 912 began in April 1965, but 2 of the 13 prototype 901s were four-cylinder models, indicating that Porsche had been studying the feasibility of this model for a few years. *Porsche AG*

THE NUMBERS GAME—
HOW DO A 901 ENGINE
PLUS A 901 TRANSMISSION AND A
901 BODY DESIGN ALL ADD UP TO A 911?

The story as to how the new Porsche model that debuted as the 901 at the 1963 Frankfurt Auto Show suddenly became the 911 only a month after production began in September 1964 is, given that the French were involved, not that difficult to understand. What is more confusing is the internal numbering system used by Porsche that assigns numbers, like 901, to a wide range of projects that can include engines, transmissions, and complete car models with similar numbers.

Let's deal with the 911's French connection first. Porsche announced that it had begun production of its new 901 model at the Paris auto show in September 1964. Upon hearing this, the good people at Peugeot claimed that they had the exclusive right to market cars in France with model numbers that had a zero as the middle digit. They had been doing this since 1929 and had a French trademark to back them up. While a larger auto maker may have raised their middle finger in response to Peugeot's middle digit claims, Porsche felt that substituting a one was much easier than trying to overcome French logic, at the risk of alienating a viable market for its latest model. The switch was made in October, 1964 but not before 82 "901" models had rolled through the assembly line.

Internally, Porsche kept the 901 designation for the engine and transmission, and other parts, used in what was now the 911. But why was the 901 so called in the first place?

When you go back to the beginning of Professor Ferdinand Porsche's engineering firm in 1930, you find that a confusing project number system was established with job one, which was labeled Job Number 7, that number being selected so that clients wouldn't think they were dealing with a firm that had no experience. With the precedent set, the numbering of subsequent projects, especially during the war, continued to be haphazard. Only six numbers in the 400 series were used. The firm started off at 500 when it reestablished itself in Stuttgart in 1949. After that, the record keeping became more structured until work began on the model that was to succeed the 356.

Porsche skipped over most of the 800 series to get to 901 as the number of the 356 successor. At the same time, a decision was also made to label all the components of a given model car with the same prefix. Prior to that, each design project, be it an engine, a transmission, or a chassis type, was given a separate number according to the sequence of when it was first drawn up.

As to why Porsche decided to go with the 900 series of numbers for cars beginning with the 901, according to Karl Ludvigsen in his in-depth study of the company, Porsche, Excellence Was Expected, it was to integrate itself with the parts control system used by Volkswagen. Porsche was moving closer to an alliance with Volkswagen and the only number series left in the VW system was the 900 range.

Of course, this still leaves the future of Porsche numerology a mystery, now that the latest evolution of the 911 bears the internal code 996.

Father and son (Ferry Porsche, left; Butzi, right) check out the dual exhaust setup on a test vehicle in 1968. The dual exhaust never made it to the production line vehicles. Both Ferry and his son took a "hands-on" approach to the development of their cars. Ferry Porsche was able to combine the engineering talent he inherited from his father, Ferdinand Porsche, with shrewd marketing skills to make the proper decisions regarding changes to the 911. That the 911 has been able to not only survive, but continue to excel in performance for over 30 years is a tribute to the brilliance of Ferry and his son, and to the basic design they laid down. *Porsche AG*

Butzi Porsche wanted to add a Cabriolet version to the 911 but was forced by the company's desire to keep production costs as low as possible to come up with a more creative alternative for open air motoring. The rollbar added occupant protection along with structural rigidity to the Targa. *Porsche AG*

built to be driven and enjoyed by their enthusiast owners, not to serve as sacred relics handed down from the heavens. And it was something other than divine inspiration that prompted Butzi's next iteration of the 911, which was unveiled two years after the coupe at the 1965 Frankfurt Auto Show. Well ahead of his time in addressing the issues of rollover safety and security for open-top cars, Butzi conceived the Targa (Italian for shield) version of the 911. A folding, rubberized removable center top section, brushed stainless steel roll bar, and a zippered, plastic rear window gave drivers the option of *al fresco* motoring without sacrificing the rigidity of the unibody or their protection if the car turned over. Butzi had to stray a bit from the elegant roofline he laid down for the coupe, although the result was no less sensational.

First put into production in December, 1966, the Targa became a big hit with customers, but given his choice, Butzi would have preferred to have drawn up a cabriolet version of the 911. Production issues forced him to come up with the alternative that would

an anomalous bit of trim or equipment fitted at the factory, say a Talbot racing mirror in lieu of the round Durant style, that shows the human touch of cars built by hand in a small family-run company. Of course, such discoveries can wreak havoc in the perfectly ordered universe created by some of the more anal retentive Porsche experts who sometimes forget that these cars were originally

not require as many changes to the body structure. The Targa took one more step farther from being a cabriolet in 1968, when a fixed glass rear window was offered as an option. This was in response to complaints that the plastic rear window was prone to scratch and crack, in addition to being hard to zip in place. The glass rear window became standard in 1969 models, although the

The 1967 911S shows off the classic curves of the 911 shape as penned by Butzi Porsche. Weighing only 2,272 pounds in street trim with a 2.0-liter engine that can be modified to make over 200 horsepower, the 1967–68 911S is a favorite of vintage racers. The 1968 models, which never were imported to the United States, do have a slight weight advantage for racing, as their chrome trim pieces were made of a lighter material than the prior year. *P. C. Paternie*

The 1968 911S engine was the same as the 1967. The 1,991-cc, single overhead cam flat six featured a 9.8:1 compression ratio, Weber 40 IDS carburetors, forged light alloy pistons, and a three-into-one heat exchanger exhaust system. It made 160 horsepower at 6,600 rpm.

Interior of 1967 911S shows leather-wrapped steering wheel, roomy flat floor, and five-gauge instrument panel that placed tachometer squarely in front of driver's view. Like the exterior, this would remain essentially unchanged until the 996. *Les Bidrawn*

Next Page: The 1967 911S (Super) featured a 160-horsepower 2.0-liter engine, 4.5Jx15-inch Fuchs alloy wheels, Koni shocks, ventilated disc brakes, a 15-millimeter front antiroll bar, and a 16-millimeter rear antiroll bar. The Fuchs alloys became legends in their own right, appearing on 911s until the late 1980s. A new 1967 911S cost $6,990. A little over 2,000 were built. *Les Bidrawn*

The 1969 911S had a 170-horsepower engine and wider, 6Jx15, Fuchs alloys. It also had mechanical fuel injection replacing the Weber carburetors of the earlier 911S. This was the last year for the 2.0-liter engine. New for 1969 was the 911E (*Einspritzung* is German for fuel injection), which had a 140-horsepower fuel-injected engine and a self-leveling, hydropneumatic front suspension. The 911T, which was not available as a U.S. model in 1968, became the base model 911 in all markets. U.S. prices were: 911T coupe, $5,795; E coupe, $6,995; S coupe, $7,695. Going with a Targa added $620 to the price of each model.

"soft window" remained as an option for that model year.

An interesting footnote to Porsche history is that one of the first Targa models built, on December 21, 1966, was also the 100,000th Porsche. This particular car was a "police special" equipped with a flashing signal light on the driver's side of the roll bar and an air raid shelter-sized siren mounted below the rear window. The hood said "POLIZEI" in bold letters. Much to the chagrin of European speeders, Porsche would build more of these specially equipped Targa patrol cars over the years.

As startling and trendsetting as the new Targa was, it was the introduction, also in 1967, of another 911 version that would become the stuff

The first year for 911s with a longer wheelbase (by 2.4 inches) to improve handling was 1969. This is the 911S. Rear trailing arms were lengthened to move rear wheels back without relocating engine. Dual batteries were installed in front fenders to further enhance the car's balance.

of legends and establish the Porsche as a world-class sports car. The 911S was powered by a high-revving version of the 2.0-liter that had bigger valves, larger Weber carburetors, forged light alloy pistons, soft nitrided forged steel connecting rods, and a 9.8:1 compression ratio (the base engine compression ratio was 9:1) to put out 160 horsepower at 6,600 rpm as opposed to 130 horsepower at 6,100 rpm. The hotter engine stretched the torque curve by 1,000 rpm over the base version, to develop 132 ft-lbs at 5,200 rpm.

Other items that set the S (for Super) above the garden variety 911 were Koni shock absorbers, a larger (15-millimeter) front antiroll bar, a

25

leather-rimmed steering wheel, basket-weave trim on the lower dash, and, despite the sporty extras, a weight saving of 154 pounds, to tip the scales at 2,272 pounds. The S also carried a number of "firsts." It was the first European car to have ventilated front brake discs, oddly enough, trailing what Porsche enthusiasts consider to be the less-sophisticated Corvette in pioneering this technology. (In 1965, the Corvette became the world's first car to be so equipped). The 911S was equipped with a 16-millimeter rear antiroll bar, the first one fitted to a Porsche road car. And last, but leaving the longest impression, were the five-spoke, forged alloy Fuchs wheels. These were 5 pounds lighter than the stock steel wheels but still measured a skinny 4.5Jx15 inches. It wasn't until the 1968 911S, which was never offered as a U.S. model, that 1-inch wider Fuchs wheels were fitted.

Original Targa models in 1967 had plastic (soft) rear windows that could be unzipped for more airflow. Owner complaints about scratches and recalcitrant zippers led to a fixed glass rear window option. In 1969, the glass window became standard, but this 1969 911S was special ordered with soft rear window.

Those skinny tires, a relatively short wheelbase, and about 406 pounds of engine hanging behind the rear wheels, when combined with the 160 horsepower, limited exploring the handling prowess of the 911S to a small group of very skilled drivers. But anyone who could stomp on the accelerator and shift gears could enjoy the giant sucking sound of a

Air vents were added to the Targa bar in 1969. Green tinted glass also became standard that year. When the original buyer of this 1969 911S opted for the plastic rear window instead of fixed glass, he was probably more concerned with maximum ventilation than what a rarity his car would be 30 years later.

In addition to the plastic rear window on this 1969 911S, the car features special order lipstick-red checked seats. The interior of all 1969 911s featured a new ventilation system with a three-speed fan and storage compartments under the armrests of both doors.

pair of triple-choke Webers with their throats wide open plus the shriek of the timing chains and all those other internal forged bits of steel and alloy furiously pumping their way toward 7,000 rpm. This was a decade before the Turbo appeared, but the thrill factor was very close. Everything seems under control approaching 5,000 rpm, about when a normal engine reached its peak, then—*Wham!*—the 911S leaps to life, rushing forward with a high-pitched wail.

Car and Driver magazine's test driver did a 0 to 60 time of 6.5 seconds. The 911S would reach 90 miles per hour in third gear on its way to a top speed of 140. *Road & Track* reported that the 911S was "everything a Porsche should be—and more." More than 30 years later, you will find that after driving a 1967 911S, or one of its immediate successors through the 1973 model year, many Porsche enthusiasts still agree with *Road & Track*'s assessment.

The endearing charm of the 911 is that despite being over 30 years old, the early cars can be driven as hard, or harder, than they were when they were new. Many parts from later models can be easily retrofitted for added durability, handling, and speed. Surprisingly, relatively limited production and exotic performance has not boosted market values of the early cars beyond the reach of the average enthusiast.

The last of what the Porsche connoisseurs called the "early 911s" (before so-called safety bumpers altered the front and rear appearance) was the limited edition Carrera RS. This rare silver model was actually yellow the first time it left the factory. One year later, its owner brought it back for a color change. Also rare are the factory installed road lights mounted on the hood. The lights were an option that was ordered primarily for cars used in rallies or night racing.

THE 1970s
PEAKS AND VALLEYS ON THE EVOLUTIONARY CURVE

The introduction of the S model in 1967 established the 911 as one of the world's top GT cars. Good news for most of the world, but the big island known as the United States has always had its own ideas about what automobiles should and shouldn't be. And just one year after the S revved its way into the hearts of enthusiasts, growing concern over automotive emissions and safety in the United States, Porsche's biggest market, made the S an illegal alien.

For 1968, all U.S. buyers could get was a basic 911 and a neutered version of the 911S known as the 911L. The L (Lux) had all the optional S goodies but with the base 130-horsepower engine in the tail. Tacked on cars bound for the United States were safety side marker lights and an air pump to control emissions. Things improved in 1969, when the S returned along with the new 911T and 911E, all on a longer wheelbase. But 1968 was a harbinger of the low point for U.S. 911

enthusiasts, from 1975 to 1978, when performance and reliability suffered while various methods were tried to control emissions, before catalytic converters and oxygen sensors came on the scene. Until the world decided that cleaner air and safer cars were not such bad ideas after all, U.S. Porsche enthusiasts, especially in California, had to accept compromises to the 911's performance. Starting in 1975, even the handling of U.S. 911s was compromised by the "5-mile per hour bumper" law that raised the ride height to conform. This lasted until the 1983 model year.

But going back to 1969, before the bureaucrats became involved with suspension settings, the emphasis was on improving the handling of the 911. To take some of the twitchiness out of the handling, beginning with the 1969 models, the wheelbase of the 911 was stretched by 2.4 inches to bring it up to 89.4 inches overall. This was done by increasing the length of the rear trailing arms to move the rear wheels back without relocating the

During the late 1960s, Porsche developed special performance packages that could be fitted to the 911 for racing and rallying. For 1967, a run of 22 lightweight (1,800-pound) cars called the 911R became the first in a long line of 911s that took basically stock cars and modified them for racing by using lightweight body parts and high-performance engines. In 1970, as the stock 911 engine grew to 2.2 liters, Porsche was well within the GT racing rules to further increase cylinder bore from 84 to 85 millimeters for a slightly increased displacement of 2,245 cc. Dual ignition, aggressive cam timing, bigger valves, and a 10.3:1 compression ratio produced 240 horsepower at 7,800 rpm. This engine, in a lightweight body, propelled the 1970 911 driven by Bjorn Waldegard to his second win in a row at the prestigious Monte Carlo Rally. It was the third win in a row for a 911, and made Porsche the first manufacturer to have such a win streak in the event's 39-year history. *Porsche AG*

The lightweight 911S also had big fender flares to clear 7-inch wheels up front and even bigger 9-inch wheels used at the rear. The best part about these rocketships was that anyone with $15,574 in 1972 could walk into the factory at Zuffenhausen and drive one away. *Porsche AG*

Special lightweight 911S models, referred to as the S/T, were prepared by the factory for racing. Plexiglas side and rear windows, fiberglass trunk lids, front fenders, and bumpers, plus aluminum-skinned doors got weighted down to under 2,000 pounds. The 2.4-liter production engine was increased to 2,494 cc, and with fuel injection put out 275 horsepower at 7,900 rpm. Note the location of the oil filler door on the right rear fender of this 1972 model. *Porsche AG*

The stock 1972 911S engine displaced 2.4 liters (2,341 cc). It had mechanical fuel injection and an 8.5:1 compression ratio, and made 190 horsepower at 6,500 rpm. The red fiberglass fan shroud is an easy way to spot the S engine. The 911E engines had green shrouds, while the T models were either black or yellow. *Matt Stone*

While the 2.4-liter 911S with its 190 horsepower was making a lot of noise at the upper end of the scale, the bread-and-butter portion of the 911 line-up, the 911T, starting midway through the 1973 model year, became the first Porsche to use the new Bosch K-Jetronic (CIS) fuel injection system. This would become standard on all 911s in 1974. It produced 140 horsepower versus 130 for the carbureted version used in Europe.

The infamous flap for external oil filler that caught unwary fuel attendants off guard during the 1972 model year. Porsche engineers had relocated the tank in front of the right rear wheel for additional handling balance. After problems with people assuming it was a gas tank filler, the tank was moved back to its original location, and the flap removed, for the 1973 cars. This is the most obvious visual difference between the otherwise mechanically identical 1972 and 1973 911 models.

The 1973 911T could be ordered with all S options except, of course, the engine. Steel spoiler was part of the package. Only U.S. models for 1973 had large rubber front bumper guards.

engine. The front and rear wheel openings were flared slightly to accept larger wheels and tires, which on the 911S were now 6Jx15-inchers with 185/70VR15 tires. Another move to improve handling was the installation of twin 12-volt batteries mounted in the fenders ahead of the front wheels. The thought was to improve weight distribution toward the front of the car and achieve balance between the left and right sides of the car.

Joining the 1969 911S (now with mechanical fuel injection that raised horsepower to 170) in its return to the United States, were two other 911 variants. The 911T (Touring) was the basic model equipped with a carbureted 110-horsepower engine and 5.5Jx15-inch wheels. The 911E (Einspritzung is the German word for fuel injection) had a 140-horsepower fuel-injected engine and the same wheels and tires as the S. The distinguishing

At the rear, the unique rubber bumpers of 1973 cannot detract from the elegant classical lines penned by Butzi Porsche. The large rubber protuberances only appeared, front and rear, on 1973 911s sold in the United States. They were Porsche's quick-fix attempt at meeting the impact safety requirements that came into effect for that model year. In 1974, to better meet the 5-mile per hour impact requirements of U.S. bumper laws, Porsche would reshape both the front and rear ends of the 911.

feature of the 911E was its front suspension, which consisted of self-leveling hydropneumatic struts in lieu of torsion bars. This was a joint effort by Boge and Porsche that was continued as standard equipment on the E until 1972. Unfortunately, the system was prone to leaks and in some cases total collapse. Most of the 911Es on the road today have been converted back to the tried-and-true 911 setup of shock absorbers and torsion bars.

Porsche effectively increased the cylinder bore of the flat six to 84 millimeters, also enlarging the engine size to 2.2 liters for the 1970 and 1971 models. Power increased across the board

Timeless beauty, the early 911 silhouette in the form of a 1973 T. A coupe like this would set you back $7,960 in 1973, plus the cost of the S options. Equipped with the CIS K-Jetronic fuel injection, the 1973 T still makes a great daily driver that does not require the constant attention of carbureted or mechanically injected models.

Unique two-tone interior (most cars were ordered with solid color interiors) sets off the Light Ivory exterior of a 1973 911T with the S option package. The car also has the optional air conditioning featuring underdash vents. Note the dual storage pockets mounted on door panels that were on 1969 to 1973 cars. These were changed in 1974, along with the use of high-back bucket seats to replace the more traditional low-back models that are reminiscent of the 356.

with the T now having 125 horsepower, the E up to 155 horsepower, and the S motor making 180 horsepower.

The zenith for the early models of the 911, and for the 911 overall according to the purists who feel later models traded some of the raw edginess of a sports car for the cushiness of a luxury GT, came with the introduction of the 1972/73 cars. Engine size went up to 2.4 liters, thanks to an increase in stroke to 70.4 millimeters, and all models got a forged crankshaft. Compression ratios were lowered on U.S. cars to meet the requirement for unleaded fuel, but the U.S. T received mechanical fuel injection. Fuel injection gave the U.S. T a 10-horsepower advantage, 140 horsepower versus 130 horsepower, over the T models in the rest of the world. The E now made 165 horsepower and the 911S a whopping 190 horsepower. The S also sported a steel front spoiler.

In January 1973, U.S.-spec T models became the first 911s to use Bosch K-Jetronic (CIS) fuel injection. Horsepower stayed at 140,

continued on page 40

SHIFTLESS IN STUTTGART:
THE SPORTOMATIC TRANSMISSION

It seems odd that a car representing the mechanical incarnation of Steve McQueen's bad boy racer attitude should provide for clutchless shifting, but the 911 has offered some form of automatic transmission throughout most of its production life. The Tiptronic has been available since January 1990 and has even made the option list of Porsche's latest Turbo. Thanks to microprocessors and other assorted bits and bytes, the Tiptronic gives up little, if any, discernible performance to a manually shifted car. In the new Turbo, for example, the five-speed Tiptronic is just 0.7 seconds slower from 0 to 60 miles per hour and tops out at 185 miles per hour as opposed to the six-speed manual's top speed of 189 miles per hour. That's with a factory test driver working the clutch. Depending on the quantity of left feet you possess and how adept you are at using them to shift gears, your times, as the small print says, may vary to a point of negligible difference.

Long before sophisticated electronics made the automatic transmission a close competitor to a manual stick shift, Porsche engineers had devised the Sportomatic transmission, which was a capable, if not comparable, alternative. Porsche had begun experimenting with automatic transmissions on the 1961–1962 356B. Having the United States as its biggest market, Porsche felt that offering some form of automatic transmission was a marketing necessity.

The Sportomatic was first offered as a $280 option on the 1968 911, including the 911S. It continued as an option, although a lack of interest dropped it from S models in 1970, until it was canceled after the 1980 model year. Part of its demise could be blamed on the change made in 1975 that eliminated a forward gear to make it a three-speed. Porsche made the change, which resulted in slower acceleration times, to decrease engine sounds in order to meet stricter drive-by-noise standards for various countries. In the early years, as proof that Porsche did understand its customers in America, it was installed on almost 25 percent of the cars delivered to the United States.

Technically, the Sportomatic was a semiautomatic transmission. It consisted of a conventional four-speed synchromesh gearbox (the synchromesh, shift collars, and shaft bearings are identical to the manual Type 901 transmission), a hydraulic torque converter made by Fichtel & Sachs, and a single-disc clutch. The clutch was operated by vacuum-controlled linkage that was set into motion by an electric switch at the base of the shift lever. According to road testers of the day, this switch was extremely sensitive, so the driver had to be mindful of only touching the gear lever when he or she intended to shift gears.

The shift knob bore the legend of P (Park) and R (Reverse) to the left of a conventional H marked with L, D, D3, and D4. Porsche suggested that L was only for "ascending or descending steep grades, or for driving on sand or ice." D was selected for normal starts with D3 and D4 as "driving gears" depending on traffic, terrain, and road conditions. Depending on how much shifting you were willing to do, you could start in any one of the four gears.

When *Motor Trend* tested a 1968 Sportomatic 911L the testers recorded acceleration times from 0 to 60 miles per hour starting in D only, D3 only, D4, and L, then shifting through the remaining gears. The results were times of 13.3 seconds, 16.1

seconds, 19.7 seconds, and 10.7 seconds respectively. Road & Track recorded 0 to 60 miles per hour in 10.3 seconds for the 1968 911L as compared to a similar car equipped with a five-speed manual that did it in 9.0 seconds flat. The bigger difference, due to gear ratios and torque converter slippage, was in top speed, which maxed out at 117 miles per hour for the two-pedal car, versus 132 miles per hour for its manually shifted counterpart. The Sportomatic was able to post closer comparative numbers when it came time to measure fuel economy. Surprisingly, fuel mileage was similar for both cars, the Sportomatic returning 16–19 miles per gallon against the manual's 15–20 miles per gallon.

The Sportomatic triggered a disparity of opinion among journalists. The road testers at the European magazines were generally more open-minded about the Sportomatic than their American counterparts. British magazine Motor said getting the most out of driving the Sportomatic required a "Porsche mentality" versus an "automatic mentality." Auto Italiana found in track testing a 130-horsepower Sportomatic versus a manual shift 160-horsepower 911S that on certain sections the automatic was a second faster due to less time lost shifting gears.

The finding came as no surprise to Porsche, as the Sportomatic's debut was at the 1967 Marathon de la Route. This consisted of 84 hours of racing around both the North and South loops (17.58 miles per lap) of the Nurburgring. The Sportomatic was fitted to a lightweight 911 with a 175-horsepower engine, essentially one of the first 911R models. The car covered 6,148 miles at an average speed of 73.15 miles per hour over the tight and twisty circuit, to capture overall honors based on a handicap system.

Even a tough guy like Steve McQueen could appreciate a gutsy performance like that.

This 1973 advertisement for the Sportomatic transmission stressed its winning debut in the 84-hour-long Marathon de la Route run over the entire old Nurburgring circuit. A complete lap included both the North and South loops for a total of 17.58 miles. Three 175-horsepower 911s equipped with Sportomatic transmissions were entered in the 1967 running of the Marathon. The winning 911 completed a distance of 6,148 miles with Vic Elford, Hans Herrmann, and Jochen Neerpasch all taking turns behind the wheel.

The 1973 Carrera RS debuted the 2.7-liter version of the flat six. Mechanical fuel injection and an 8.5:1 compression ratio were good for 210 horsepower at 6,300 rpm. The engine's increased capacity was achieved by changing the bore of the 2.4-liter 911S engine from 84 millimeters to 90 millimeters. Otherwise the two engines were essentially the same. *Autocar* magazine tested a Carrera RS Touring in 1973 and got a 0-to-60-mile per hour time of 5.5 seconds. The quarter-mile time was 14.1 seconds, and top speed was 149 miles per hour.

Porsche began listing its options with an "M" prefix in 1970. One of the most famous was the 1973 M471 code, which stood for the Carrera RS Sport, a lightweight version of the 911S, intended for club racers. Thinner gauge steel was used in the body panels along with thinner window glass; insulation, carpeting, rear seats, and other interior trim were all deleted. Recaro sports seats, a ducktail rear spoiler, and larger wheels and tires (6x15 with 195/60 front, 7x15 with 215/60 rear). Only 200 of the sport versions were made, and they sold for $10,200. Option M 472 was the Carrera RS Touring, a more deluxe version that was equipped similarly to the standard 911S; 1,308 of the Touring version were made. U.S. price was $11,000.

The fiberglass over an aluminum frame deck lid with ducktail spoiler is the most distinguishing characteristic of the 1973 Carrera RS. On later production cars, the aluminum was replaced with steel framing. Larger rear wheel flares and 7-inch-wide rear wheels also differentiate its exterior from a 1973 911S. The "1st RS" on the license plate of the car pictured represents that this particular car (Serial Number 911 360 0016) made the first public appearance for the Carrera RS on the stand at the Paris Salon in October, 1972, when Porsche debuted the RS model. The car also went on to be displayed at auto shows in Geneva and London. Its first owner purchased the car directly off the floor of the London show.

Continued from page 35

but the improved operation and low maintenance (versus tinkering with carburetors or the mechanical injection) of this system, along with excellent fuel economy, make these cars excellent drivers even today.

One change Porsche made to the 911 for 1972 was not as well received and disappeared on the 1973 cars. The dry sump oil tank was relocated from a position behind the right rear wheel to a spot ahead of it. In conjunction with this move, an external filler door was placed on the right rear fender to allow oil to be added without going into the engine compartment. Porsche engineers moved the oil tank to further enhance the handling balance of the 911. Unfortunately, unwary filling station attendants mistook the outside oil filler for the fuel door. This happened often enough to prompt Porsche to move the oil tank

For 1974, the Carrera RS 3.0 and RSR models carried the Carrera RS theme to further extremes. Whale tail rear wings replaced the smaller ducktail for increased stability at high speeds. There was also a big change under the rear spoiler, as the RS 3.0 had a 3.0-liter engine replacing the 2.7-liter unit for a 105-horsepower increase.

A special fleet of 15 cars were built and sold to Roger Penske to be driven by world class racers like Mark Donohue, A. J. Foyt, the Unsers, Bobby Allison, Richard Petty, and others in the initial round of the International Race of Champions, or IROC as it was nicknamed. The 3.0-liter (2,994-cc) engine in these cars produced 315 horsepower at 8,000 rpm.

back to its old location, sans the filler door, on the 1973 cars. The tank used in 1973 was made of stainless steel.

In addition to the ill-fated oil filler flap, other ways to differentiate between the nearly identical 1972 and 1973 cars are the rectangular exterior mirrors, black trim surrounding the taillights and front indicator lights, and black plastic front air intakes on the later year cars.

Another big change for 1972 was the introduction of the Type 915 transmission, derived from the Type 916 transaxle used in the 908 race car, that was needed to handle the increased power output (torque) of the enlarged engines. The original Type 901 was distinguished by a "dogleg" first gear which was to the left and down from the H pattern of the four higher gears. A good pattern for racing, but one that had the occasional 911 street driver starting out from lights in second gear. The 915 moved first to the top of the H in the more conventional arrangement with fifth now being up and to the right. Reverse selection went from being forward from first on the 901 to down from fifth on the 915. The

In 1974, the Carrera took over from the 911S as the top-of-the-line regular production 911. In RoW trim, its 2.7-liter engine still made 210 horsepower. Emissions controls limited the U.S. Carrera to 170 horsepower. The 911 hood decals were optional in 1974 and 1975 but not very popular for obvious reasons.

915 was also designed for use in a four-speed format, which was part of the standard equipment package for the 1972 911.

The 915 transmission featured improvements over the 901 in terms of increased spacing between the input and output shafts, along with better bearings, beefier gears, upgraded synchromesh, and a pull-actuated clutch release bearing.

The 1973 model also saw the debut of the limited production, lightweight Carrera RS model, powered by a larger 2.7-liter, 210-horsepower engine. Lean and mean, the Carrera RS is considered by many Porsche enthusiasts to be the quintessential 911.

From the high-water mark established by the 1973 911S and Carrera RS, things tailed off rapidly for U.S. cars, beginning in 1974. The classic "face" of the 911 that Butzi said defined a Porsche in the eyes of the world was altered to include protruding aluminum bumpers with accordion-like, rubber bellows, to meet government requirements regarding 5-mile per hour impact protection and absorption. The good news was that the 2.7-liter engine that debuted in the Carrera RS was now fitted with Bosch K-Jetronic (CIS) fuel injection and installed in all 911s, but the bad news was that its power was significantly reduced. The T and E models were replaced by the base 911 with 150 horsepower and the 911S, which had 175 horsepower. The Carrera was no longer a special model but a regular production car assuming the top-of-the-line role of the S. Emissions controls limited its power to 175 horsepower. The rest of the world still enjoyed Carreras with 210-horsepower mechanically injected engines.

Fitting new safety bumpers not only affected the exterior of the 911, it reduced trunk space, which led to the elimination of the twin batteries. A larger, single battery now resided at the rear of the trunk.

There were some improvements. Revisions were made to the suspension. Forged aluminum trailing arms, 7.7 pounds lighter, were used in the rear while up front, a simpler method of mounting the antiroll bar was used. It no longer passed through the inner fender walls, but beneath the body pan.

Inside, high-back seats with integral headrests added a more modern look to the 1974 911, which also benefited from an improved interior ventilation system.

By 1975, ever tightening emissions laws had created California and 49-state cars, both versions suffering from diminished horsepower ratings. The U.S. Carrera was more bark than bite. European versions of the Carrera still produced 210 horsepower at 6,300 rpm, while the U.S. cars put out a puny 165 horsepower at 5,800 rpm. *Porsche Cars North America*

This 1974 factory photo shows workers installing the Sportomatic on 911s. It was a $425 option. Close to 25 percent of early 911s delivered to the United States were equipped with the transmission but its popularity dwindled, along with its gearing, which went from four forward speeds to three, through the 1970s until it was dropped from the option list in the 1980 model year. *Porsche AG*

In 1975, U.S. 911s were divided into 49-state cars and California cars depending on the emissions controls fitted. In addition to an air pump, California cars had thermal reactors and exhaust gas recirculation (EGR) systems. As stated above, the next three years, with the exception of the 1976 debut of the 260-horsepower Turbo, was a dismal period for U.S. 911 enthusiasts.

Things began to brighten when the 3.0-liter 911SC came on the scene in 1978. Horsepower increased to 180 for all markets, including California—good news after 1976 models in the state had been choked down to 160 horses. Wider rear fender flares on the SC allowed Porsche to upgrade the standard wheel and tire package. Fitted up front were 6Jx15 wheels with 185/70VR15 tires, while 7Jx15 wheels with 215/60VR15 tires were slipped under the larger rear fender openings. Power brakes became standard on all 911s. First time options included 16-inch wheels, 6J in front and 7J at the rear.

Having survived the last half of the 1970s, the 911 was poised to make a strong comeback in the 1980s.

From special order to a special production model in 1987, factory Slant-nose Turbos (referred to as the 930S in the U.S.) were a status symbol of the 1980s until a rash of cheap knock-offs eroded their unique appeal.

THE 1980s
THE SURVIVAL AND REVIVAL OF THE SPECIES

By 1980, the 911 had adapted fairly well to the ever increasing safety and emissions regulations that had threatened to strangle its performance in the latter half of the 1970s. The larger 3.0-liter engine of the SC, though limited to 180 horsepower in the United States, was good for 0 to 60 times of 6.3 seconds, according to a 1978 Road & Track test. It was also more reliable than the previous 2.7-liter, which was never designed to accommodate the heat and stress associated with the U.S. emissions controls that had been adapted to it. With the 3.0-liter powerplant and a body made of galvanized steel, introduced on the 1976 models, the 911SC held the promise of a long and healthy future.

Unfortunately, that was a promise that could have been broken if Porsche's CEO at the time, Ernst Fuhrmann, had had his druthers. Fuhrmann believed that the 911 had run its course and that it should be phased out. He wanted marketing and development efforts concentrated on cars like the 924 and 928. Fuhrmann, who in his early days as

an R&D engineer had designed the legendary four-cam Carrera racing engine used in the RS Spyders, had been appointed to top management in 1971. Ferry Porsche decided that to avoid family squabbles over who should run the business, it would be better if the limited partnership (consisting of Porsche and Piëch family members) that controlled the company was changed to a public corporation. Family members were to give up significant management roles, a decision that precipitated both Butzi Porsche and Ferdinand Piëch to leave the company to successfully pursue their goals elsewhere. One would be foolish to find fault with Ferry Porsche's reasoning at the time. It was an ironic twist of fate that in doing what he believed to be the best move for the company's future, he set in motion a plan that would eliminate from that future the two men who had inherited the vision and enthusiasm that he shared with his father. Porsche went public in 1973.

Fuhrmann had been a big supporter of the 911 in the factory GT racing programs of the 1970s, but

The 911SC was a step forward for the 911, signaling that Porsche could build a performance car and still meet the world's demands for safer and cleaner cars. Basically, Porsche had taken the Carrera body with its flared fenders and detuned the Carrera 3.0-liter engine to cope with the various emissions regulations in all of its markets.

by 1980 had decided the company needed to concentrate on new products. It was a scary time for 911 enthusiasts, as indicated in a 1978 911SC Car and Driver road test article written by David E. Davis. David E. wrote, "If you've never owned a Porsche, or driven one, you owe yourself the experience . . . especially since there can't be too many more years of life in the 911 series. I wouldn't want to grow old without counting a Porsche among my memories, and neither should you."

As things turned out, it was Fuhrmann, not the 911, who got phased out to early retirement in 1981. His vision of the 911's future in the Porsche product line-up was obviously not shared by the majority of Porsche faithful, inside or outside the company, as 911 sales outpaced the 928 by more than two to one. Fuhrmann's place was taken by an American, Peter Schutz, who recognized that demand for the 911 was still strong. Not only among the hardcore enthusiasts, but, more importantly, among the increasing numbers of affluent young urban professionals—call them yuppies if you like—who appreciated the social status, if not the driving rewards, that comes with owning a prestigious German sports car. Under Schutz's administration, changes to the 911 would be aimed at both groups of buyers, but the free-spending yuppies presented a bigger target. And no one could blame Porsche for firing most of its rounds in their direction. One year after the Carrera 3.2 hit the market, sales soared to over 20,000 units. Total sales for the 911SC from 1978 to 1983 were 57,972 cars in a rising economy, while its replacement, the 3.2-liter Carrera, totaled 49,629 units from 1984 to 1989 despite an economic downturn toward the end of that period. Consider too that a U.S. version 1978

911SC coupe cost $19,500 and by 1983 had risen to $29,950. The new, improved 1984 Carrera 3.2 hit the streets based at $31,960, but by 1989 even status-seeking profligates had to pause at a sticker price that had climbed to $51,205.

During the 1980s, people were paying more per pound for 911s and 911s had more pounds to pay for. A 1969 to 1973 911 weighed about 2,250 pounds. The 1978 911SC coupe tipped the scales at about 2,560 pounds. While some of that weight gain could be attributed to the safety and emissions hardware, much of it was due to additional sound insulation and comfort items such as air conditioning and power windows, which became standard on U.S. models in 1980. Power brakes and center consoles were part of the SC package. There was some nonsensical excess baggage as well. During this period U.S. cars were required to have 85 miles per hour speedometers based on the specious reasoning that drivers wouldn't be tempted to exceed that speed if their speedometers refused to acknowledge higher numbers. In other words, our government safety experts felt

Rallying was the forte of early 911s with the model's first victory being a class win at the 1965 Monte Carlo Rallye, finishing fifth overall. While the 911 had been dropped from factory road racing programs by 1980, Porsche was still committed to its use in rallying as evidenced by this photo taken at the 1981 San Remo Rally of Walter Rohrl in a 911SC. The rigors of competition, especially rallies, could provide a severe test for new engineering ideas in a day or two, as opposed to months of less strenuous road testing. During the 1981 rally season Porsche experimented with a four-wheel drive 911, a concept that would mature into the advanced system of the 959. A grueling test of the 959 ended with a victory in the 1986 Paris-Dakar Rallye. *Porsche AG*

that going real fast is no fun if you don't know exactly how fast you are going. This type of thinking wasn't confined to federal bureaucrats. A few years earlier, Porsche had decided to remove the degree scale from the oil temperature gauge so that owners would not be alarmed by the high readings on cars equipped with thermal reactors.

If you doubt that an extra couple of hundred pounds can change a car's personality, try this experiment. Hop into a 180-horsepower 1970 911S

for a quick drive. Then do the same route in a 180-horsepower SC. The latter car will still sound and act like a 911 but its reactions to steering and throttle input won't seem as sharp as the early car. You should notice that more than the engine sound is muted. Certainly the SC is more comfortable as a daily driver or weekend cruiser but on tight, twisty roads the extra padding can muffle the immediate and intense communication that is transmitted between an early 911 and its driver.

THE SLANT-NOSE TURBO:
PORSCHE'S STYLE SETTER FOR THE
DISCO ROLLER CROWD WAS, LIKE, SO 1980S

The Slant-nose Turbo exemplifies the best and worst extremes of the 911's evolutionary path through the 1980s. These cars are some of the most easily recognizable of any 911 variant, distinguished by their flat, front fenders, with louvers punched into their top surfaces, which slope down to the bumper line. At the sides, box-shaped lower doorsills taper back into wide rear fenders that are accented with gaping air intakes. Later models have pop-up headlamps. Under all this flashy bodywork sit the basic ingredients that make up a 930 Turbo with horsepower ratings stretching as high as 330 horsepower.

The first Slant-nose conversion was built in Porsche's restoration shop as a special order in 1981. From 1982 through 1987, when it then became a limited production option (M506, also known as the 930S in the United States), 235 more were turned out. In 1987, 200 930S cars came to the United States, followed by 278 in 1988, and 147 in 1989. There were an additional 50 of these production versions delivered to other parts of the world.

Looking like street versions of the 935 race cars, the Slant-nose models built by Porsche were exciting cars, whether you were outside or inside one. Riding in one, even at low speeds, feels like being strapped into the front seat of a runaway roller coaster. The illusion is of being perched on the nose of the car as the road rolls under you and the rest of the world hurtles over and around you. Check out the side view mirrors and the tips of the large rear wing look like miniature alien spacecraft pacing your progress. A very impressionable experience, even as 911 Turbos go.

Unfortunately, the swoopy looks of the Slant-nose also made a huge impression on the gold chain crowd, who felt more comfortable driving them to discos than on the racetrack. Soon, cars that began as plastic imitations of the factory's handiwork escalated into gross exaggerations. It did not take long before, in shops and garages and a few backyards all over the country, there emerged a cottage industry in which innocent 911s, and quite a few 912s, were being hacked up and "converted" into Slant-noses. Some people used metal fenders, like the factory, but usually fiberglass was the medium of choice. Imitation may be the sincerest form of flattery but when it came to Slant-nose replicas, it was a case of adding insult to the badly injured 911s and 912s used in the process.

A special Porsche model that took its cue from what Porsche does best—racing—soon became symbolic of drug dealers and other nefarious characters. Fortunately, like any fad, the Slant-nose look faded away. One rarely sees these cars today. The nonfactory cars have either been converted back to conventional looking 911s or presumably are stashed away as confiscated evidence in a large DEA warehouse in Florida.

The factory cars can now enjoy the respect that they deserve as unique 911 variants.

The major difference between the factory-produced Slant-nose and its imitators was the use of hot-dip galvanized steel fenders by the factory. The original concept for the car was the dropped nose of the 935 factory race cars that took advantage of a loophole in FIA racing regulations to gain an aerodynamic edge over the competition. Other components used by the factory Slant-nose conversion option were retractable headlights, air vents along the top of the front fenders, rocker panel fairings, air scoops with horizontal ridges (strakes) in the rear fenders, an oil cooler with a cooling fan mounted in the rear air scoop, and, on European models, an increase of 30 horsepower over the standard 300-horsepower Turbo engine. Randy Leffingwell

In 1986, 959s finished first and second in the Paris-Dakar 8,000-mile-plus rally. A special four-wheel drive version 911, with a 230-horsepower engine, had won the event in 1984. For the 1985 attempt, Porsche used a hybrid that mated the 959 chassis to a nonturbocharged powerplant similar to that used in 1984, but with less than successful results. For 1986, the cars entered were true 959s with twin-turbo engines that put out 390 horsepower and the four-position drive selection system of the road model. Rene Metge, who had driven the 1984 winner, repeated the feat in 1986. Jacky Ickx, more famous for his winning Porsche drives at Le Mans, was second. Porsche engineer Roland Kussmaul, who served as the team manager and chief mechanic, drove a third 959 to sixth overall. *Randy Leffingwell*

This communications breakdown between car and driver may explain why amplifiers and other bits of stereo gear suddenly began populating the trunks of 911s during the 1980s.

Another example of the sybaritic path chosen by the 911s of this decade was the Weissach Edition of 1980. In the 1960s and 1970s, limited editions, like the 911R or Carrera RS, usually deleted comfort items to pare down weight while adding a combination of larger wheels and tires with more powerful engines to raise the performance level. The 408 Weissach models produced for the United States in 1980 took a different tack. They were distinguished by a choice of either Black Metallic or Platinum Metallic paint, full leather interiors, Fuchs alloys painted to match the body color, power antenna, power sunroof, fog lights, and a passenger side exterior mirror. The only addition that could be considered as a performance improvement was the mounting of the whale tail rear spoiler from the Turbo.

51

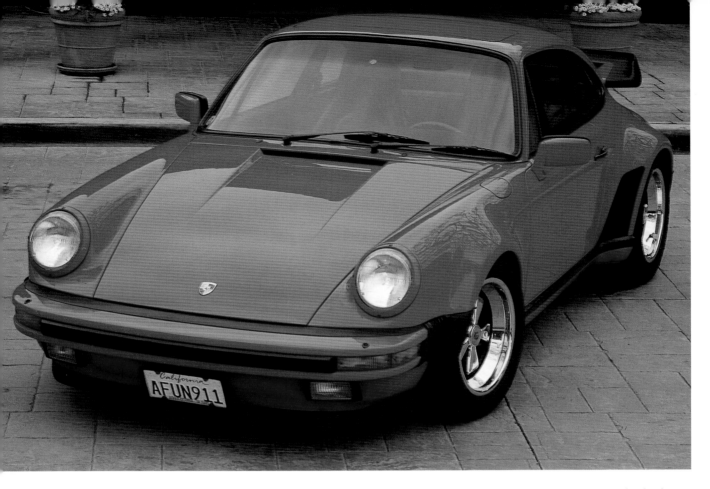

A popular option on Carrera 3.2 models was the Turbo Look. You actually got more than just the look. Besides the bulging flares and front and rear spoilers, Porsche also included the big brakes, big wheels (7- and 9-inch widths, front and rear), rear torsion bars, and antiroll bar of the Turbo.

In 1983, for its final year of production, the SC did add a distinguished accomplishment to its resume before bowing out to the Carrera 3.2. The first factory edition of the 911 Cabriolet, essentially a Targa with the roll bar removed and replaced by a folding alloy frame covered with a three-layered convertible top, made its debut as a 911SC. In the United States, a 1983 Cabriolet, with manual top, was priced at $34,450 while the Targa listed at $31,450.

The Carrera 3.2, while continuing to add more comfort and convenience touches during its production run, reenergized the performance side of the 911 as well. The 3.2-liter engine was essentially the same in all markets except for the compression ratio and emissions equipment, which was determined by whether a market used leaded or unleaded fuel. In the United States, Canada, and Japan this meant using pistons that gave a compression ratio of 9.5:1, while what Porsche

Turbo Look was only available on coupes until 1986, when it became available also for Targas and Cabriolets. Cars looked fast and handled better than a "narrow" body car, but 110 pounds of Turbo fat hurt acceleration a bit.

Porsche brought another name out of the past to boost sales in 1989. A limited production run of Cabriolets with cut down windshields, humpbacked fiberglass rear seat tonneau covers, and low-slung convertible tops were called Speedsters. Here a couple of the 2,065 built go through final assembly. *Porsche AG*

Reflections of the past made the Carrera Speedster a "must have" for collectors when it first came out. The sticker price for a 1989 Speedster was $65,480 but the cars have not become the sought-after collector's car that many who paid that or more when the car came out had anticipated. Neither faster nor better looking than the regular production Cabriolet, the 911 Speedster lacks the cult appeal of the original 356 Speedster. As a no-frills roadster, the seats, windows, and top all operate manually. The 911 Speedster top

was not as well fitted or insulated as on the Cabriolet. Porsche advised customers not to run the car through an automatic car wash. Customers were also asked to sign a statement accepting increased wind noise and the possibility of water leaks when the top was in place. The top's most endearing feature was that, when raised, it covered the hunchback rear seat cover. There were 823 Speedsters made to U.S. specs. Of the 2,065 total cars produced, 1,894 were fitted with the Turbo Look body.

The 959: Porsche's Exotic 911

Porsche engineers and enthusiasts have always taken pride in what can be achieved by taking a production-based 911 and turning it into a race car. In 1983, at the Frankfurt Auto Show, Porsche took the wraps off the 959 to let the world take a peek at what could be accomplished with a 911-based race car turned into a street machine. It also offered a glimpse up the road that future 911s would travel, as many of the 959's technical and styling traits have evolved into the regular production versions from the 964 to 993 to 996.

Powering the 959 was a twin-plug, 24-valve, double overhead cam, 2.85-liter (2,849-cc), flat six-cylinder with sequential twin turbos, Bosch Motronic fuel injection, and water-cooled heads that were derived from the 956 engine. This combination was good for 450 horsepower at 6,500 rpm. With a drag coefficient of 0.32 and weighing around 3,200 pounds in street trim, the 959 could go from 0 to 60 miles per hour in about 3.6 seconds and top out around the magic 200-mile per hour mark.

The 959 featured a six-speed manual transmission, an electronically adjustable suspension, ABS brakes, and 17-inch hollow wheels (8-inches wide in front and 9-inches wide at the back) equipped with sensors to detect low tire pressure. The main attraction, of course, was the electronically controlled four-wheel drive system that could vary power distribution from front to rear, based on road conditions. The driver could select from four automatic drive programs including: dry road, wet road, ice and snow, and full traction.

Although it served as a dramatic engineering showcase, Porsche's decision to build the 959 was not to serve as a concept car, but as a race car. Building 200 road-going customer versions of the car not only meet the Federation Internationale de l'Automobile (FIA) regulations for the Group B rally class it was designed to compete in, but also defrayed some of the development costs.

Following the lead of the all-wheel drive Audi Quattro in 1981, a car developed by ex-Porsche R&D chief Ferdinand Piëch, the Group B rally cars had earned the nickname of "Killer Bees" for their extremely high-speed capabilities on dirt trails and forest roads. Speeds and danger to spectators and drivers increased as

Although the 959 spent very little time on the race track compared to other high-performance variations of the 911 theme, it is considered by many to be the ultimate 911. At the time of its introduction, the 959 pioneered such innovations as sequential turbochargers, electronic fuel injection and turbo boost control, six-speed transmission, all-wheel drive, and speed-dependent ride height adjustment. Its 450 horsepower and top speed of 196 miles per hour are still high water marks for production 911s. Randy Leffingwell

other manufacturers followed Audi's lead in all-wheel drive. Unfortunately, the Killer Bees would live up to their nickname in tragic accidents that led to changes in the rules before the 959 was ready to compete.

Helmut Bott, Piëch's successor at Porsche, had been experimenting with four-wheel drive 911s starting in 1975. In 1984, he entered a three-car team made up of four-wheel drive variants of the 911SC rally car, with normally aspirated 3.3-liter engines, in the grueling Paris-Dakar raid, the event so named because it resembled desert warfare more than a rally. Finishing 1st, 6th, and 26th, Porsche decided to return in 1985 with cars decked out in 959 bodywork and an early version of the 959 drivetrain, again excluding the turbo motor. A lack of horsepower prevented the Porsches from winning. For 1986, Bott entered three full-on 959s, which resulted in a 1-2-6 victory that proved to be the 959's competition high point. The road racing version of the 959, known as the 961, did race at Le Mans twice in 1986 and 1987. It won its class in 1986, finishing 7th overall. The 1987 effort had a more dismal ending, as the car caught fire after blowing its engine.

Ironically, as things turned out, at a price close to $200,000 a copy when the car was ready for market in 1986, the sold-out production run of 959s proved to be a bigger commercial than racing success for Porsche. The exotic car market was booming during the 1980s, trying to satisfy the needs of the serious hardcore enthusiasts as well as the self-indulgent appetites of the "Me Generation" and its attendant speculators. The limited availability and 200-mile per hour capabilities of the 959 played right into this market. A good example was the on-again, off-again delivery plans for Environmental Protection Agency- and Department of Transportation-approved versions of the 959, which drove sticker prices to at least $300,000 for cars that could not legally be driven in the United States. Porsche lore says that at least four of these cars were imported, but no definitive answer is available. More than a decade later, the legal issues of owning and operating a 959 in America have not been resolved.

Despite its limited competition success and the circumstances surrounding its commercial success, the 959 stands tall as a technical tour de force. Almost 20 years later, its performance is still state of the art and its mechanical attributes, allowing for the dramatic progress made in computer controls, still qualify as world class.

referred to as the Rest of the World (RoW) engines had a compression ratio of 10.3:1. Both numbers were up from the 3.0-liter SC engine, which in 1978 had a compression ratio as low as 8.5:1 across the board. From those of the 3.0-liter SC engines, horsepower numbers took a dramatic leap upward, as RoW engines soared to 231 from 204 horsepower. U.S.-spec cars broke the 200-horsepower barrier for the first time ever, if you exclude the 210 horses that powered the limited edition 1973 Carrera RS. The performance leap over the SC by the U.S. Carrera 3.2 cars because of the jump from 180 to 204 horsepower was a dramatic one in spite of an added 110 pounds that brought their weight to 2,670 pounds.

A big part of the 3.2-liter engine's performance advantage could be attributed to having the first application of the Bosch Motronic 2 DME (Digital Motor Electronics) engine management system combined with LE-Jetronic fuel injection. Improved oil-fed chain tensioners, henceforth known as "Carrera tensioners," were also a major feature of the 3.2-liter engine.

Other performance enhancements on the new Carreras included larger and thicker brake discs front and rear (11.8-inch diameter and 12.1-inch diameter, respectively) and, in 1986, thicker antiroll bars, measuring 22 millimeters (front) and 21 millimeters (rear) were added, along with rear torsion bars that increased in size from 24 millimeters to 25 millimeters.

Bodywork was essentially the same as the SC with a new front spoiler that incorporated fog lights. Sixteen-inch wheels (7J front, 8J rear) were optional. A popular option was the Turbo Look that essentially added the fender flares and spoilers from the Turbo along with its suspension, brakes, tires, and wheels.

On the luxury side, the Carrera 3.2 had its radio antenna integrated into the windshield, vanity mirrors in the sun visors, leather seats as standard on U.S. cars, and central locking as standard starting in 1986. Power seats and mirrors became standard equipment in 1988. In 1987, Cabriolet models all came equipped with power-operated tops.

The 959 combined all-wheel drive, ride height adjustment, and turbocharging to become a super 911. It was not built for off-road superiority as an FIA Group B rally car, but for what Porsche had hoped would become a sports car road racing series based on Group B regulations. Porsche, required to make at least 200 road versions of the 959 to meet the FIA homologation requirements for a production car, produced a total of 284. Two versions of the road car were offered. The standard 959 came complete with power windows, air conditioning, and rear seats, while the lighter-weight 959 Sport, intended for club racing, deleted those items. Lightweight construction involved using a number of materials, including galvanized steel for the basic body structure, aluminum for doors and trunk lid, reinforced fiberglass for the front fascia, and an aramid composite for rocker panels, roof, and fenders. Despite these efforts, the fully equipped road version of the 959 weighed 3,194 pounds, considerably more than its 2,423-pound minimum weight for racing. *Randy Leffingwell*

Basic philosophy and outline of the 911 changed very little from 1965 to 1984. However, safety and emissions regulations, and consumers who demanded more comfort and luxury in their performance cars, resulted in big changes during the first 20 years of production. A 300-pound weight gain was offset by 101 more horsepower. Evolution can be costly as price also increased—from $6,500 to $31,960. *Porsche AG*

Another big change occurred in 1987 when the Type 915 transmission was replaced by the Getrag-built G50 five-speed with Borg-Warner synchromesh. The 915 had reached its torque limit and required its own oil cooling system. The G50 was a cheaper alternative. With the new transmission, 911 drivers seeking reverse had to get used to moving the lever to the left and up as opposed to going right and down. With the G50 also came a larger (240-millimeter, like the Turbo) clutch, which was now hydraulically operated.

In 1989, 16-inch wheels were standard along with an alarm system. But prices had risen from $31,960 in 1984 to $51,205 for a 1989 coupe. By then U.S. sales had plummeted from a high of 7,801 cars in 1987 to 3,377 in 1989. A special run of 1989 Speedster Cabriolets accounted for 823 more U.S. cars, along with 7 lightweight Club Sport limited edition models, but an economic downturn had curbed the spending appetites of yuppies. And those who still could afford a Porsche were ready to trade in their sports cars and join the trendsetters driving SUVs.

Speaking of trends, an interesting one had developed regarding U.S. Cabriolet sales. In 1984, Cabriolet sales were roughly half that of the Targa model which, in turn, sold in equal amounts to the Coupe. By 1987, the Cabriolet moved ahead of the Targa in sales. For that year, Coupe sales were 2,916; Targas 2,232; and Cabriolets 2,653. In 1989, Porsche sold 1,361 Cabriolets in the United States, compared to only 860 Targas. At the time a Cabriolet listed for $59,200 while a Targa cost $52,435. In addition, 823 more convertibles were sold as limited edition Speedsters, with a price tag of $65,480.

The Speedster was a marketing effort by Porsche to boost sales by reviving the memory of one of its most famous models. What was really needed was a model that looked to the future, not the past. Porsche felt it had such a model in its first attempt at a "new 911," the Type 964. Following the example of Porsche's limited production supercar, the exotic 959, the 964 series had the four-wheel drive Carrera 4 as its flagship to lead Porsche and the 911 into the 1990s.

The 2000 Carrera coupe carries a slicked-back version of Butzi Porsche's 911 silhouette into the twenty-first century. Propelling the new Carrera into the future is something that Butzi didn't imagine, a liquid-cooled 3.4-liter flat six with direct coil-over-plug ignition and self-adjusting hydraulic valve lifters. It still sits behind the rear axle as Butzi intended. *Porsche Cars North America*

THE 1990s
EVOLUTION OR REVOLUTION?

ype 964, 993, then 996. Could any of these numbers equal 911? During the last decade of the century, Porsche was hard at work on finding the right equation for making a 911 that would appeal to the past, present, and, most importantly for the company's profitability and survival, future owners. One of the big discoveries the company made was that it is hard work to keep a living legend alive. Butzi Porsche grappled with the same problem when he started doodling designs for the original 911 to pick up the torch from the 356. A good measure of how difficult such a task can be is that Porsche went into the 1990s with the Type 964, which was billed as a "new 911" and came out of the 1990s with the New 911 (Type 996). In between came the 993, which, largely because it is the last air-cooled engine model, many Porsche purists consider the ultimate evolution of the 911 design as conceived by Ferry and Butzi Porsche. So Porsche made three tries in a little over 10 years to settle on how

much history they had to lug down the road to the future.

Let's examine the first of the "new" 911s. Internally it was called the Type 964, but it came to be more commonly known as either the Carrera 2 or Carrera 4 models depending on which drivetrain was used. The 964 qualified for distinction as a "new 911" because, even though it looked similar to the 911s that had been coming out of Zuffenhausen since 1963, Porsche claimed that 87 percent of its parts were new. The roof, front fenders, trunk lid, doors, and seats were all carried over from the previous model so the 964 still bore a strong resemblance to the old 911. Underneath the old 911 look, however, the engine, suspension, brakes, and drivetrain were all "new 911" technology. The Carrera 4, which went into production in January, 1989, could also be called an evolution of the 959 because Porsche's all-wheel drive supercar, and its Paris-Dakar rally-winning 961 siblings, served as the

Porsche revived the Carrera RS name in 1992 with special lightweight club racer specials for European customers. The United States and Canada got the RS America instead. The U.S. cars weighed 2,955 pounds, as opposed to the European Carrera 2 RS, which tipped the scales at 2,712 pounds. Deleted to save weight were air conditioning, power steering, power sunroof, sound insulation, and rear seats. The sunroof and air conditioning could be ordered as options.

inspiration for building a regular production model with four-wheel drive. Porsche had been experimenting with four-wheel drive systems for the 911 since 1975 and displayed a four-wheel drive 911 at the 1981 Frankfurt Auto Show. The system that went into the 964 was a new system and not the same as that of the 959. The four-wheel drive Type 964 Carrera 4 hit the market as a 1989 model with Carrera 2, the rear-wheel drive only version, joining it for the 1990 model year.

The four-wheel drive system of the Carrera 4 comprised a five-speed gearbox, based on the G50, that transferred power to a front differential via a rigid torque tube that carried a central driveshaft. A transfer case split engine torque, with 31 percent directed to the front wheels and 69 percent to the rear. ABS wheel sensors were used to detect wheel spin and redirect torque (up to 100 percent) from front to rear or vice versa as needed. The gearbox of the 964 carried the designation G64/00.

Driving all those wheels was more new and exciting technology. Increasing the bore and the stroke of the previous 911's 3.2-liter six, Porsche engineers came up with a 3.6-liter engine that produced 250 horsepower for all of the markets, including the United States. The last time U.S. cars were on equal horsepower footing with the Rest of the World was in 1978, and that came about by decreasing RoW horsepower. With the new 3.6-liter, everybody shared in the power gain. RoW horsepower ratings went up from 231

The RS America was powered by the stock Type M64/01 3.6-liter 250-horsepower engine, which ran on 95 RON unleaded fuel. The Carrera 2 RS had the Euro-spec M64/03 motor, which ran on 98 RON unleaded fuel to make 260 horsepower. The factory claimed a 0–62-mile per hour (100-kilometer per hour) time for the RS America of 5.4 seconds and a top speed of 162 miles per hour, the same as for the Carrera 2 RS. The Type M64/01 engine was the same as in the regular production Carrera 2/4, with a 100-millimeter bore and a 76.4-millimeter stroke, for an even 3,600-cc capacity. Other features were a twin-spark ignition system with dual distributors, antiknock sensors, a 12-blade cooling fan, and cylinder heads with ceramic port liners for cooling efficiency.

horsepower while U.S. customers gained a whopping 33 hp!

A twin-spark ignition system, knock sensors, and a new Motronic engine management system with sequential fuel injection were the major components responsible for the across-the-board power increase, catalytic converters installed or

Andial converted 25 of these cars to full Carrera Cup specs; they had to be reconverted once the series was canceled. All of the cars were Grand Prix White with black interiors, except one that was painted Guards Red.

The RS America came with sport seats, while the Carrera Cup car had stock seats. RS America weighed 2,955 pounds, thanks to deletion of air conditioning, power steering, sunroof, sound insulation, and rear seats. However, for RS America buyers, air conditioning, stereos, and sunroofs were popular options, which negated much of the weight saving over a Carrera 2.

The RS America in these photos is fitted with aftermarket racing wheels. Standard wheels on RS America were 17-inch Cup Design alloys measuring 7 inches wide in front and 8 inches wide in the rear. Carrera Cup car has wider 17-inch Cup Design alloys that are 7.5 inches wide up front and 9 inches wide in the rear. Most notable visual difference between the RS America and U.S. Carrera Cup car is the large rear spoiler on the RS America, in lieu of the moveable stock unit retained on the Cup car.

not. A 12-blade cooling fan, ceramic port liners, and a revised cylinder wall design kept things cool enough to make the 964 the first 911 without an engine oil cooler. And starting with 1993 models, Porsche also switched to the use of synthetic motor oil.

An even bigger departure from Porsche's past was the suspension of the new Carrera 2/4.

Gone were the torsion bars, victims of the space requirements of the four-wheel drive system. MacPherson struts were retained up front with new cast-aluminum lower arms. The rear was suspended by cast-aluminum trailing arms with coil-over shocks. More bad news for the purists, the increased forward weight of the new drive system necessitated

Porsche claimed that the 993 had 80 percent new parts, compared to the Type 964 that it replaced. The exterior only carried over the roof and hood of the previous model. Underneath the altered body panels were major changes to the suspension and drivetrain. Gone were the traditional semi-trailing arms at the rear. The LSA (Light, Stable, Agile) multi-link suspension that replaced them was more driver friendly through turns, decreasing susceptibility to drop-throttle oversteer. This was a good idea, since out back was a more powerful 3.6-liter engine putting 272 horsepower through an equally new six-speed transaxle.

Narrow waist and bulging fenders along with revised bumpers gave the 993 more visual appeal than the model it replaced. As the last air-cooled 911, many consider it the highest evolution of Butzi Porsche's initial concept.

The taillights and bumpers of the 993 evoke more of the classic 911 look than the bulky rear end styling of its predecessor the 964. The moveable rear wing, which was first introduced on the 964, carried over to the newer model. The wing pops up at speeds over 50 miles per hour to improve high speed handling and as the car slows to around 6 miles per hour, the wing lowers itself back into place on the rear deck lid. Depending on the whim of the driver, the rear wing can also be raised or lowered when the car is standing still by a switch on the console.

Modern interior look of this 993 is enhanced by gray-and-blue leather with titanium-colored gauge faces. Driver and passenger airbags became standard in all markets, which prompted Porsche to update the interior's appearance and improve heating and air conditioning systems. Traditional five-gauge setup was retained but a rainbow of colored information screens lurked behind them, ready to educate or warn the driver as necessary.

the installation of power-assist to the rack-and-pinion steering.

It was too little, too late to save his job, but Ernst Fuhrmann had to be delighted to know that at least part of the 928 progressed into Porsche's future product line. The brakes fitted to the Carrera 2/4 were derived from the 928 S4 and featured all-wheel ABS. The five-spoke Fuchs alloy wheels that had so long been associated with the 911, since their debut on the 1967 911S, were retired in favor of modern 16-inch alloys. Called Club Sport wheels, they have seven short spokes

and large, convex centers that may be more aerodynamic but are certainly less visually exciting than the Fuchs wheels. In 1992, a more attractive option, the five-spoke Carrera Cup wheels, became available.

Speaking of good looks, the appearance of the 964 reverses the axiom that "beauty is only skin deep." With all of its advanced technology, it looks better below the skin. The thermoplastic body-colored front and rear bumpers and lower side sills may have been more aerodynamically efficient but gave the 964 a lumpy, unfinished

The 1999 Carrera 4 brought all-wheel drive to the 996 model line-up, in coupe or cabriolet body styles. The new system incorporated a viscous clutch, which moved from the gearbox location of the 993 to the front differential housing for better weight distribution. Power, anywhere from 5 to 40 percent depending on conditions, is transmitted to the front wheels via drive shaft in the frame tunnel. Porsche Stability Management (PSM), which uses a combination of traction control, braking, and engine management to reduce oversteer, was also part of the Carrera 4 package. Externally, the only way to spot the 1999 Carrera 4 is by its unique 17-inch wheels and the titanium color of the name badges and brake calipers. *Porsche AG*

The 996 has all the amenities of a contemporary luxury car, including the navigation system. Five-speed Tiptronic S and all-wheel drive of the Carrera 4 add a sophisticated level of high performance without disrupting the luxury image. *Porsche Cars North America*

look. One could be extremely unkind and say that these pieces looked more like the plastic cladding one would expect from Pontiac, not Porsche.

The evolution of 911 styling has always been a good example of form following function, and, despite the bumpers and side trim, the 964 did make a significant evolutionary contribution. In a concession to retaining the elegant slope that Butzi had penned for the rear of the 911 while improving high-speed stability, the rear wing of the 964 was designed to raise and lower itself into the engine lid depending on the car's speed. The wing would pop up as speeds exceeded 50 miles per hour and drop out of sight when the car decelerated below 6 miles per hour. No one can say if the engineers involved with its development considered the possibility of it being used as incriminating evidence in traffic court.

Another part of the 911's past was recalled in January 1990 when the Carrera 2 offered the option of a four-speed automatic transmission. The Tiptronic, like the old Sportomatic, could either be shifted manually or used in a full automatic mode. A Tiptronic-equipped Carrera 2 was about 1.0 second slower from 0 to 60 miles per hour than a manual shift model.

Establishing itself as leading edge in safety as well as performance, the 1990 United States version Carrera 2/4 was one of the first cars to come with dual air-bags as standard equipment. In 1991, all left-hand drive 964s were so equipped.

All this technology had its price. At $58,500 for a C2 coupe, the 964 cost over $7,000 more than the car it replaced. The four-wheel drive added another $11,000 to the sticker and well over 200 pounds to the vehicle's weight. At 2,970

pounds, the Carrera 2 was already 300 pounds heavier than the previous Carrera 3.2. Despite the added weight, thanks to the big increase in horsepower, the C2 managed to shave about a half second off its predecessor's 0 to 60-mile per hour time, clocking in at 5.6 seconds.

Porsche may have billed the Carrera 2/4 as the "new 911," but no one was buying it, literally. Hitting U.S. showrooms just as the country was heading for a major economic downturn, sales of the car were dismal. In the 1993 model year, the last full year the car was produced, there were about 1,700 cars sold in the UnitedStates and a quarter of that total was a special 450-car run of lightweight RS America models. Besides having a slight performance advantage, the RS America listed at $53,900, a substantial price advantage over the regular production coupe. Another special edition, the Carrera 2 Speedster in 1993, was not as well received. Porsche planned to make 3,000 of the Cabriolets with cut-down windshields and humpbacked fiberglass covers over the rear seats, but only 936 were ever built. Just 427 of these were U.S.-spec cars.

At this point in time, it not only looked again as if the 911 might become extinct, but

THE TARGA
TAKES COVER

As pointed out in Chapter 3, by 1989, Cabriolet sales were outpacing those of the Targa by almost two to one. This trend increased with the Type 964. In 1991, Porsche sold 2,207 Cabriolets and only 746 Targas. Worldwide sales figures had a similar ratio, with 3,886 Cabriolets being produced versus 1,196 Targas. Sales of all the 964 models fell drastically until production stopped at the end of 1993, but Cabriolets continued to outpace Targas by more than three to one.

When the 993 took over from the 964, the Targa version was conspicuous by its absence. In 1996, Porsche brought back the Targa, but it was much changed from the concept Butzi had unveiled in 1966. Built on a Cabriolet chassis, the new Targa had the appearance of a coupe with a huge, tinted skylight. The skylight was actually a glass panel that could, at the push of a button, slide back and under the rear window. The panel was insulated and coated to filter out ultraviolet rays to avoid creating a greenhouse effect in the cockpit. For added protection, a screen could be rolled out to further cut down on sunlight.

While the rest of the world was intrigued enough by this concept to cause Targa sales that first year to give the Cabriolet a run for the money, 1,980 Targas to 2,066 Cabriolets, U.S. customers still bought 2,152 Cabriolets versus only 462 Targas. In 1997, U.S. sales had similar results while in the rest of the world, Cabriolets outpaced Targas by 400 units. There were reports of leakage and some people complained about the view out the rear when the top glass was lowered next to the rear window.

The Targa was not part of the original 996 line-up but is expected to return, possibly as soon as the 2001 model year.

Watching the 996 convertible top going through its paces can be a crowd-pleasing experience. Operated by a push button on the dash, the top raises or lowers itself in 20 seconds. Part of the show includes the deck behind the rear seats, which raises itself up as the top folds back into a recess behind the seats. This area is covered up as the deck drops back into place. An aluminum alloy hardtop, weighing just 73 pounds is easily installed for extreme winter weather conditions.

In 2000, the 996 engine got a performance bump to an even 300 horsepower, thanks to new exhaust system. Other changes include a soft-touch grain dashboard and interior trim. Aluminum accents on the shift knob, handbrake handle, and inside door handles are a nice touch that also livens up the interior. *Porsche Cars North America*

Porsche, at least as an independent company, might also disappear. The next 911, the 993, did turn out to be the last air-cooled 911, but as such it successfully bridged the gap between the original 911 concept and what was needed for Porsche and the 911 to be viable entities in the twenty-first century. The muscular styling of the 993, almost a macho caricature of Butzi's original design, won back the purists put off by the bulkiness of the 964. Only the roof and trunk lid were carried over from the 964.

The 993 retained the 3.6-liter engine, but lighter pistons and connecting rods with an upgraded engine management system raised the power level to 272 horsepower. Hydraulic lifters were added for quieter running and to reduce maintenance. The 993 chopped 0.3 seconds off the 0 to 60 miles per hour of the 964, stopping the clock at 5.4 seconds.

A new rear suspension marked the most radical departure of the 993 from past 911s. A multi-link system replaced the semitrailing arms used on previous models. Called LSA—Lightweight, Stable, Agile—the suspension consisted of a two-piece cast-aluminum transverse-mounted arch to which were attached dual wishbones, also of cast-aluminum. The main advantage of LSA was a decrease in the 911's long-familiar propensity for

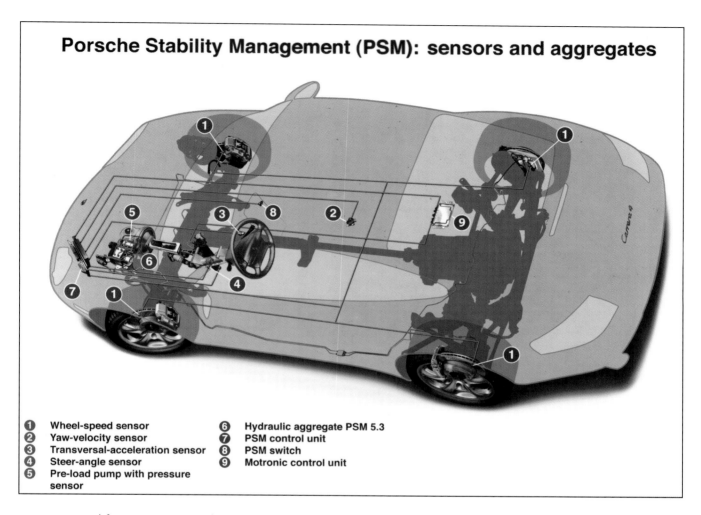

Porsche Stability Management (PSM): sensors and aggregates

1. Wheel-speed sensor
2. Yaw-velocity sensor
3. Transversal-acceleration sensor
4. Steer-angle sensor
5. Pre-load pump with pressure sensor
6. Hydraulic aggregate PSM 5.3
7. PSM control unit
8. PSM switch
9. Motronic control unit

Optional for 2000 on rear-drive models is the Porsche Stability Management System (PSM), which can detect a loss of grip at either end of the car and compensate by braking the appropriate wheel, or, if needed, by altering engine power. *Porsche Cars North America*

Next page: In 1999 and 2000, Porsche declined to field a factory-based effort to race at Le Mans for the overall win. The company wanted to devote all of its engineering talent and budget to developing a Sport Utility Vehicle. It relied on its customers to represent the Porsche name using the 996-derived 911 GT3R. The normally aspirated water-cooled 3.6-liter six-cylinder puts out 420 horsepower. The GT3R did win its class at Le Mans 2000, a class in which all of the entries were Porsches.

PORSCHE 911 GT1:
THE ULTIMATE RACING 911

When a Porsche 935 won the 1979 24 Hours of Le Mans, it seemed a pretty safe bet that this would be the last 911-derived car to ever win the classic endurance race. At the time, even the production 911's future looked bleak. Twenty years later, the 911 is still going strong and has added a 1998 victory in France by the 911 GT1 98LM to its family album.

After years of domination by sports prototype racers that bore little resemblance to road-going cars, the overall victory at Le Mans in 1995 by the racing version of a McLaren F1 exotic road car created interest among other manufacturers to build similar cars. According to Le Mans rules, these cars competed in the GT-1 category for limited production sports cars, which, although they were race cars, could theoretically be offered in street versions. Porsche decided that it would build such a car, based on the 911, for the 1996 Le Mans race.

The carbon fiber constructed exterior silhouette of the GT1 was unmistakably that of the 911, but it was also part 911 under the skin. The front end of a 993, back to the B pillar was used as part of the chassis. The 3.2-liter, twin turbo, liquid-cooled engine was derived from the 911 flat six. Power

in Le Mans trim was rated at 600 horsepower at 7,200 rpm. A six-speed gearbox, ABS, and power steering were also part of the package. From the rear, above the twin air diffusers were a familiar-looking pair of 911 taillights.

The GT1 was a success in winning the GT-1 class at Le Mans in 1996. In 1997, the GT1 was leading overall at the 22-hour mark when the car caught fire and burned. For 1998, Porsche upped the ante of its GT1 by building the entire body and chassis of carbon fiber, to shave about 250 pounds off the car's weight. A longer tail and swoopy new fender lines added 7 inches in length while the car also became wider and an inch lower, to improve speed and handling down the Mulsanne Straight. The 3.2-liter, twin turbo, four-valve engine with TAG 3.8 engine management system looked the same on paper as its predecessor, but benefited from tuning tweaks derived from the 996 program.

Whatever Porsche did, it worked, as a pair of GT1 98LMs finished one-two in an exciting race that featured a duel with the favored Toyota GT-One, which was not decided until the final hour. Besides the victorious driving team of Allan McNish, Stephane Ortelli, and Laurent Aiello, 911 fans around the world had reason to celebrate. The 911 had won Le Mans again and fittingly, as Porsche's most successful model, in the company's 50th anniversary year.

Porsche's GT1 was introduced in 1996 after the FIA instituted rules for a GT class based on production-based sports cars, of which only one road-going example needed to be made. Porsche had to move quickly in order to enter such a car for Le Mans that year, so it used the front end of a 993 attached to a conventional racing chassis. It also used the water-cooled version of the flat six engine, producing 600 horsepower, mounted ahead of the rear wheels for optimum handling balance. The GT1 project was completed in eight months. The two cars entered at Le Mans in 1996 finished first and second in class, and second and third overall to a Porsche prototype car. Similar cars ran less successfully at Le Mans in 1997 and in the FIA GT world championship series.

snap oversteer when the driver lifted abruptly off the throttle while cornering. LSA also controlled rear end squat during acceleration.

The 993 featured larger ventilated and cross-drilled brake discs up front, 12.0 inches in diameter, while the ventilated and cross-drilled rear rotors remained at 11.8 inches in diameter. Four-piston calipers were used at all four wheels. An improved ABS system was part of the package. The ABS sensors also functioned as part of the Automatic Brake Differential (ABD) option, available on cars with manual transmission, to detect wheelspin at the rear wheels upon acceleration. Selective braking was then applied performing a function similar to a limited-slip differential.

A new six-speed manual transmission was part of the new 993 package, or buyers could choose an optional improved version of Tiptronic.

To complement its more aggressively styled body, Cup Design 93 wheels, with spokes designed to draw hot air off the brakes at speed, were standard equipment. Wheel sizes were 7Jx16 inches up front and a wider 9Jx16 inches in the rear.

The Type 964 remained in production through December 1993. Production of the 993 began in January 1994 as part of the 1994 model year. Porsche sold nearly 15,000 993s that year, and nearly 18,000 the next year. That was 1995, which saw the debut of the 993 Carrera 4 with a redesigned all-wheel drive system. The new system used a viscous coupling and central shaft to send power to the front wheels and weighed about half as much (111 pounds) as the computer-controlled system of the 964. ABD traction control was standard on the new Carrera 4.

Also beginning in 1995, Tiptronic customers could order the Tiptronic S version, which included thumb switches on the steering wheel in addition to the console-mounted lever for selecting gears in the manual mode.

For 1996, a variable length (via sliding runners) intake system, called Varioram, was added to the 3.6-liter engine. Horsepower increased to 282 horsepower, most notable in midrange performance, while fuel consumption and emissions were reduced. A distinctive siren sound above 5,000 rpm let the world know that Varioram was at work.

As good as the 993 was, and it is still highly regarded by 911 fans some of whom prefer it to the latest model, only so much can be done to improve on a design that stretches back to the late 1950s. It was time for a New 911. And Porsche was able to deliver it in the form of the 996.

Though its appearance has been criticized as being a bit too bland, especially following the Rubenesque lines of the 993, the shape of the 996 brings the evolution of Butzi's classic 911 curve to a state-of-the-art, aerodynamically efficient conclusion. Porsche did make the mistake of grafting the 996 nose on the Boxster, which preceded the 996 to showrooms, a move that opened the door for complaints that the shape of the latest 911 is not distinctive enough. Critics also argued that the 911 should not share body and mechanical components with a lower priced "entry level" Porsche.

What established the 996 as the New 911 as opposed to a "new 911" was the change from an air-cooled engine to one that is liquid-cooled. In order to keep up performance, and keep engine heat under control, while meeting stricter noise and emissions requirements around the world, Porsche was forced to make the switch. Making 296 horsepower at 6,800 rpm, the latest flat six develops more horsepower than the 993's air-cooled unit, despite moving down in displacement from 3.6 to 3.4 liters. Dual overhead cams operate four valves per cylinder. VarioCam (variable valve timing) adjusts intake valve timing for maximum breathing efficiency whether at high or low rpm. Also on board is the latest iteration of Varioram, Porsche's two-stage induction system. Previous systems relied on sliding intake runners while the latest version uses a butterfly valve to match intake pressure to rpm. Fuel economy is up, and 0 to 60 times are down, to 5.2 seconds, compared to the 993.

The new engine required a stronger six-speed gearbox, which has a cable-actuated shift mechanism and is worked by pedals that are hinged from the top, not from the floor as on all previous 911s and 356s. A reworked five-speed Tiptronic S now has five computer maps that adapt the automatic shift points to match the driving style of whoever is behind the wheel.

The front and rear suspensions have been modified to take full advantage of a chassis that has been stiffened by 50 percent, yet weighs 154 pounds less. The wheelbase has also been extended by 3.2 inches to measure 92.8 inches overall. Larger brakes have also been fitted front and rear. Seventeen-inch wheels, 7 inches wide in front and 9-inches wide at the rear, are standard equipment, with 205/50ZR and 265/35ZR tires fitted, respectively. Optional wheels are 7.5Jx18 and 10Jx18.

Harm Lagaay, Porsche's chief designer, said his goal was to design "a car that would have the clear lines distinguishing all Porsches of the 356 and 911 ancestral line." He had aerodynamic goals, as well as ancestral ones, to meet. As a result, the windshield rake of the 996 has been laid back from the 60-degree slant of its predecessors to a more airflow-efficient 55 degrees. Better integrated bumpers, repositioned side mirrors, and a slipperier underbelly have given the 996 a drag coefficient of 0.30. The retractable rear spoiler now pops up at 75 miles per hour and assists the 996 to a top speed of 174 miles per hour.

The longer, wider body and more efficiently packaged engine have also made the 996 roomier inside.

Is the 996, then, the perfect 911? The highest peak on the 911 evolutionary curve, it is clearly the best engineered and designed 911 so far. If it has a failing, subjective views on styling aside, it is that it is too good of a 911. The handling limits are so high and the car performs so well that it is almost too easy to drive at the speeds one can reach outside of a racetrack. At least to those to whom the 911 experience includes the constant tugging on the steering wheel to offset the feedback

A 1998 family group photo. Boxster roadster behind 996 coupe could easily be mistaken as a slightly downsized 996 Cabriolet. Note the distinctive glass roof of 993 Targa on the right. The sliding glass roof version of the Targa debuted in the 1996 model year. Lower wind noise and better rollover protection than the traditional soft-top Targa were the driving forces behind the electrically operated glass panel that was also treated to filter the ultraviolet rays of the sun. The roof added 66 pounds over the weight of a 993 coupe. The Targas were built on Cabriolet bodies. *Porsche AG*

from the changing road surface and the challenge of making throttle adjustments to keep the rear tires in line. Also missing is the raspy exhaust note accompanied by a mechanical symphony of timing chains and fan blades. The original 911 was a very visceral piece of machinery, and mastering its complexities and eccentricities was part of the experience. The 996 is comfortable and a delight to drive. But it may be a little too sophisticated and aloof to command the devotion and enthusiasm of the earlier, less perfect, examples of the 911.

Deciding which is the best 911 comes down to personal preference. Porsche has done its job of following the evolutionary curve laid down by Butzi. It is up to the enthusiast to decide how far along the curve he or she wants to go before getting off.

The Porsche Turbo once again raises the bar for rear wing style and function. The Turbo also raises the upper part of its two-piece rear stabilizer when speeds above 75 miles per hour are reached, and the wing lowers as speed decreases to 50 miles per hour. The wing aids in the flow of intake air. Rear fenders are also 2.6 inches wider on the Turbo to accommodate 18-inch alloy wheels with 295/30ZR18 tires. Air scoops in the fenders direct air to intercoolers. *Porsche Cars North America*

THE 911 TURBO
EXCELLENCE EXCEEDS EXPECTATIONS

Ernst Fuhrmann, the man who a decade later would lose the top spot at Porsche for feeling that the 911 had reached its evolutionary peak, was the driving force behind the original 911 Turbo, or 930 in reference to its internal project number. Coming up through the development engineering side of the company, Fuhrmann was a strong advocate of racing as a means to improve the breed.

Author Karl Ludvigsen in his history of Porsche, *Porsche, Excellence Was Expected*, has a quote from Fuhrmann regarding the special relationship that made racing an integral part in the design process of Porsche's road cars. It is especially poignant considering the company's recent decision to cut back on its racing program in order to use those funds to diversify its product line.

"It belongs to us, this racing business," Fuhrmann said. "We are often asked why we spend so much on it. If you design a production car, you know in five or six years what you've done. In racing, you know in a year."

What Fuhrmann knew from racing the 917 in the Can-Am series was that turbocharging an engine could extract gobs of horsepower with what he felt were very little trade-offs. That convinced him to have his engineers develop a turbocharged 911 for his personal use. The results from experimenting with a 2.7-liter engine using Bosch K-Jetronic fuel injection were encouraging enough to create a show car in this configuration for the Paris auto show in September, 1973. Ten years after the debut of the original 911 that was destined to become an automotive icon, the introduction of the Turbo heralded a version of the 911 that was to transcend being an automotive icon to become a cultural icon. Whether it was the outrageous styling or the promises of 280 horsepower and speeds of 160 miles per hour, more likely the

combination of the two, the Porsche Turbo created such a powerful image in the public eye that soon everything from laundry detergents to vacuum cleaners were being advertised as delivering "turbo- charged'"performance.

Starting in 1974, Porsche would apply turbocharged performance to its 911 racing efforts in cars like the 934 RSR and the mighty 935 that would rule world sports car racing for the rest of the decade.

The first production model of the Turbo came out in October 1974 as a 1975 model. Unlike the Paris show car, the engine was a 3.0-liter (2,994-cc) variation of that used in the Carrera 3.0. This engine was chosen over the 2.7-liter primarily because of its better low-end throttle response, which reduced some of the "lag" felt during acceleration before sufficient turbo boost built up. The Turbo engine had thicker cylinder heads than the normally aspirated

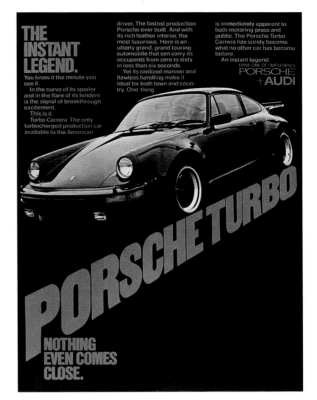

The Porsche Turbo Carrera not only was an "instant legend," with a top speed of over 155 miles per hour and 0 to 60 in 5.5 seconds, it became a cultural icon for anything outrageously fast or powerful. But it was the sudden surge of power that came on like a rocket booster around the 2,500-rpm mark and just kept going to 5,500 rpm, that created the Turbo legend.

Left: Bulging fender flares and large rear wing have been a Turbo trademark since the first ones entered the United States as 1976 models.

3.0-liter engine. The compression ratio was lowered to 6.5:1. The KKK turbocharger was mounted at the left rear of the engine. A unique feature that had come down from the racing cars was a blow-off valve controlled by manifold vacuum pressure that kept the turbo rotors spinning even if the throttle was closed momentarily. This was another way Porsche had sought to overcome turbo lag. The Turbo engine package weighed 456 pounds, tipping the scales

Sold as Turbo Carreras, the first year Turbos featured blacked-out chrome, body-colored headlight rings, headlight washers, fog lights, and power sunroof.

about 70 pounds heavier than a normally aspirated 2.7-liter unit.

Debuting in Europe, the 1975 Turbo was the first street Porsche to feature a breakerless ignition system. To handle the added torque of the turbo motor, a new transmission was designed. Dubbed the 930/30, it was a four-speed with a wider ratio set of gears that were also beefier than the ones used in the 915. A larger (240-millimeter) clutch was also part of the 930 package. Suspension changes included revisions to both the components and suspension geometry. The 15-inch Fuchs alloys of the first 930 were 7 inches wide in front and 8 inches wide in

the rear. The 930 was the first production car to make use of the new Pirelli P7 low-profile high-performance radial tires. These measured 205/50 and 225/50, front to rear. They were optional in 1975 but became standard in 1976.

While European versions of the Turbo boasted 260 horsepower at 5,500 rpm, U.S. emissions equipment, including thermal reactors, limited the power to 245 horsepower at 5,500 rpm. Good enough for Car and Driver magazine to set a clutch-searing, tire-scorching 0 to 60-mile per hour time of 4.9 seconds! The European magazines that had tested the more

The 3.0-liter engine had one KKK exhaust-driven turbocharger. When 0.8 bar boost came on, the compression ratio of 6.5:1 effectively became 11.7:1, to squeeze out 245 horsepower on U.S.-spec cars.

powerful versions had more conservative times (and launches), hovering around the 6-second range. U.S. cars were introduced in August 1975 as the 1976 Turbo Carrera. Equipped as luxury models, the Turbo Carrera's $25,850 sticker included a stereo, fog lights, air conditioning, and leather interior.

In 1978 a new 3.3-liter engine with intercooler boosted horsepower to 300 for RoW cars while the U.S. cars went to 265 horsepower.

The Turbo disappeared from the U.S. line-up in 1980 as rumors of the demise of the entire 911 range began to spread. The car continued to be sold everywhere else, averaging sales of well over 1,000 units per year.

In 1986, thanks to the magic of Bosch's Motronic DME (Digital Motor Electronics) and oxygen sensors in the exhaust which allowed the use of catalytic converters and unleaded

The Turbo interior had standard leather trim and a three-spoke steering wheel but was basically the same as the 1976 911. No boost gauge was fitted.

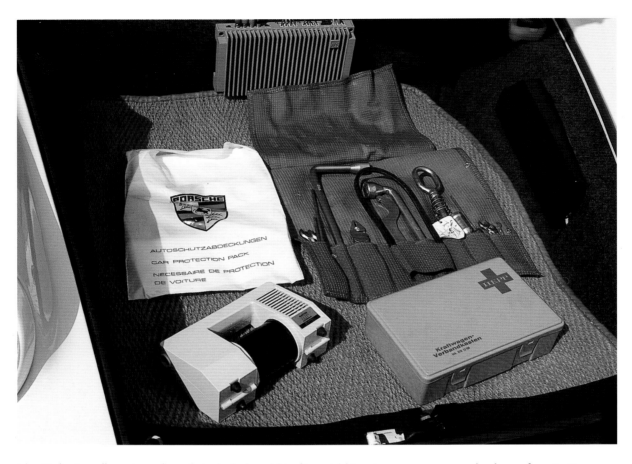

The Turbo's well-equipped trunk included tool kit, first aid kit, air compressor, and a box of protective covers to avoid scratching the car while maintenance was carried out.

fuel, the Turbo was again deemed to be worthy of reentry into the United States. For $48,000, you got 282 horsepower and 16-inch wheels that were 7 inches wide in front and a whopping 9 inches at the rear. In 1988, the Turbo became available for the first time as a Targa or Cabriolet. The good news for 1989 was that the five-speed G50 with hydraulic-actuated clutch became available. The bad news was that the change to the Type 964 in 1990 eliminated the Turbo model.

The Turbo's absence lasted only a year and it reappeared in the new 964 body style wearing a large flat rear wing. A revised exhaust system, larger turbo charger, and a larger intercooler had raised the horsepower to 320 at 5,750 rpm. U.S. models were now equal in power to the RoW cars. New 17-inch Cup Design wheels were part of the package.

The changeover from the 964 to the 993 took the Turbo model off the market again for the 1994 model year. It was back better than ever in 1995 wearing the 993 bodywork with a sleeker rear wing. Under that wing things looked even better, thanks to a new 3.6-liter engine sporting twin turbos and two intercoolers. Power was up to 408

continued on page 92

The 360-horsepower 3.6-liter engine that debuted in January 1993 retained the Turbo's role as Porsche's image model. A five-speed manual, limited-slip differential, and three-piece Cup Design 18-inch wheels were all part of the package. *Matt Stone*

The 3.6-liter Turbo engine had a 7.5:1 compression ratio and made 360 horsepower at 5,500 rpm. Space restrictions limited this engine to one spark plug per cylinder. *Matt Stone*

Below: The racecar evolution of the 911 progressed from the 1967 911R to the Carrera RS and RSR of 1973 and 1974 to the turbocharged 934 which was built to 1976 FIA Group 4 regulations. The 934 had a 3.0-liter (2994 cc) turbocharged engine that put out about 530 hp. *Randy Leffingwell*

Porsche's GT2 race car made 430 horsepower, but for $150,000 you could buy a limited edition Turbo S that had 424 horsepower and the luxury of a custom leather interior. *Matt Stone*

Porsche 911 Turbo Race Cars: Whale Tales, The Moby Dick, and More

Porsche's notoriety for producing powerful turbocharged 911s is not limited to road cars. Some of the most powerful, and creatively engineered, 911s ever produced were turbocharged racing models that ruled GT racing from 1976 to the early 1980s. Like many successful Porsche race cars, they were built by taking advantage of rules that were intended to level the playing field among Porsche and its competitors. Thanks to the engineering and interpretive genius of Porsche racing boss Norbert Singer, and much to the chagrin of sanctioning bodies and competitors, these rules had the opposite effect. For Porsche fans, Singer's talents not only provided winning celebrations but also

memorable cars like the outrageous Type 935/78 Moby Dick 1978 Le Mans car.

The Group 4 Turbo RSR was designed to meet the regulations for the 1976 international GT racing season as specified by the Federation Internationale de l'Automobile (FIA), the sport's governing body. They were called Type 934 to indicate that they were 930 (Turbo) models built to Group 4 Grand Touring Specifications. Because the 934 had a turbocharged 3.0-liter engine, it was classified by the FIA as the equivalent (1.4 times more powerful than a normally aspirated 3.0-liter engine) of a 4.2-liter car. The minimum weight for a 4.0–4.5-liter car was 2,470 pounds, or slightly less than a fully loaded 930 street car. As a result, very little weight was taken out of the 934 and of the 31 cars built, some ran with their electric windows still in place. The biggest difference that the 934 had over the stock Turbo was the use of 16-inch wheels and an air-to-water intercooler that allowed boost pressures capable of producing 500 horsepower or more. Porsche chose to limit the 934 to 485 horsepower at 7,000 rpm. The 934 was highly successful in various European GT championships as well as Trans-Am and eventually IMSA racing in the United States.

Left: The 935 started out as a leaner, meaner 2.8-liter 590-horsepower version of the 934 to conform to the less restrictive 1976 Group 5 GT class rules. By the 1978 season, Porsche racing boss Norbert Singer had read deeply between the lines of the FIA rule book to produce a GT race car that still retained the production roofline of a 911 but had otherwise become an 800-horsepower aerodynamic device. The long, sweeping rear fenders designed primarily for stability on the Mulsanne Straight, gave rise to the car's nickname of Moby Dick. They also let it reach a top speed at Le Mans of over 227 miles per hour. Unfortunately, Moby Dick failed to win the 24 Hours, but it did inspire similar efforts from privateers like the Kremer brothers, who built a 935 that won in 1979. Randy Leffingwell

As formidable a competitor as the 934 was, the 935 version, built to conform to the looser rules of the Group 5 or Special Production Car category, was even more intimidating. Because of a sliding weight scale tied to engine displacement and freer rules regarding tire sizes and suspension components, there were cars that competed as either a 934 or a 935, but Porsche did build two specific 935 cars for the 1976 season. Using a 2.8-liter engine and an air-to-air intercooler tucked into a huge rear wing, coil suspension, and 19-inch tall by 15-inch wide rear wheels, these cars were rated by the factory at 600 horsepower with available bursts of up to 630 horsepower if necessary. Testing at Paul Ricard, the 935 had had a higher top speed than a six-wheel Tyrell Grand Prix car also using the circuit. A Road & Track magazine comparison test of a 1976 935 versus a 934 had the 935 going from 0 to 60 miles per hour in 3.3 seconds while the 934 was clocked in 5.8 seconds. More impressive were quarter-mile times of 8.9 seconds against 14.2 seconds and the 935's reaching 0 to 150 miles per hour in 11 seconds flat, almost twice as fast as the 934's 21.4 second reading.

But Singer wasn't done with the 935 or the rules regarding it. For the 1978 season, he read into the regulations that defined the "body" in reference to what had to be left stock on the race car. What he ended up with was the 935/78 that had a 911 roofline and doors sitting between sloping front fenders devoid of headlights, exaggerated box-like fender flares, and a swoopy tail extension that earned the car its nickname of Moby Dick. The low-slung racer also had a 3.2-liter engine with water-cooled heads that produced 740 horsepower at 8,200 rpm. With full boost, the car produced close to 900 horsepower. At Le Mans, the Moby Dick reached 227.5 miles per hour on the Mulsanne Straight. Unfortunately, various problems kept the 935/78 from being more than an artistic success. It finished 8th at Le Mans. It did serve as the basis for future refinement by private teams. In 1979, the Kremer Brothers modified 935 won the 24 Hours of Le Mans.

Continued from page 86

horsepower, with improved low-end torque that brought acceleration times down near 4.0 seconds to travel from 0 to 60 miles per hour. Other niceties included a six-speed transmission and four-wheel drive. Wheels and tires measured 8Jx18 with 225/40ZR radials up front and 10Jx18 with 285/30ZR radials at the rear. Huge brakes (12.7-inch rotors) led to epic stopping potential. The Turbo could travel from 0 to 60 miles per hour and back to 0 in less than 6.5 seconds.

Released as a 2001 model, the 996 version of the Turbo takes this performance icon to even greater levels with a top speed of 189 miles per hour and a 0 to 60-mile per hour time of 4.0 seconds flat. Power is up to 420 horsepower at 6,000 rpm. For the first time ever, the Turbo is available with a five-speed Tiptronic as an option. It is only 0.7 seconds slower to 60 than the six-speed manual transmission. Larger brakes are also fitted, similar to the ones found on the current GT3 race car.

Not a bad way to celebrate the Turbo's twenty-fifth birthday.

Twin turbos and two intercoolers filled up all the available room in the Turbo S engine compartment. *Matt Stone*

Air scoops in the rear fenders and a sculpted rear wing make the Turbo S a visual treat from the outside, but a look inside at the yellow accents of this example is by no means a letdown. Custom leather interior trim was part of the Turbo S package. *Matt Stone*

APPENDIX

TALE OF THE TAPE:
WEIGHTS AND MEASUREMENTS THROUGH THE YEARS

Dimensions

1965–68

Wheelbase	87.0 inches
Height	52.0 inches
Width	63.4 inches
Weight	2,380 pounds
Fuel tank capacity	16.4 gallons

1969–73

Wheelbase	89.4 inches
Height	52.0 inches
Width	63.4 inches
Weight	2,250 pounds
Fuel tank capacity	16.4 gallons

1974–77

Wheelbase	89.4 inches
Height	52.8 inches
Width	65.0 inches
Weight: 911	2,370–2,470 pounds
Turbo	2,630 pounds
Fuel tank capacity	21.0 gallons

1978–83

Wheelbase	89.4 inches
Height	52.8 inches
Width	65.0 inches
Weight: 911	2,560 pounds
Turbo	2,870 pounds
Fuel tank capacity	21.0 gallons

1984–89

Wheelbase	89.4 inches
Height	52.8 inches
Width	65.0 inches
Weight: 911	2,670 pounds
Turbo	2,940 pounds
Fuel tank capacity	21.0 gallons

1990–94 C2

Wheelbase	89.4 inches
Height	51.9 inches
Width	65.0 inches
Weight: 911	2,970 pounds
Turbo	3,234 pounds
Fuel tank capacity	20.0 gallons

1995–98 993

Wheelbase	89.4 inches
Height	51.8 inches
Width	68.3 inches
Weight: 993 C2	3,014 pounds
Turbo	3,465 pounds
Fuel tank capacity	19.4 gallons

1999 996

Wheelbase	92.6 inches
Height	51.4 inches
Width	69.5 inches
Weight	2,910 pounds
Fuel tank capacity	16.9 gallons

911 Performance Chart

Model	Engine	0–60 mph (seconds)	1/4-mile (seconds)	Top Speed (mph)	Source
1965 Coupe	2.0-liter	9.0	16.5	132	Road & Track
1967 911S	2.0-liter	8.1	15.7	141	Road & Track
1968 911L/Sportomatic	2.0-liter	10.3	17.3	117	Road & Track
1970 911S	2.2-liter	7.3	14.9	144	Road & Track
1972 911T	2.4-liter	6.9	15.1	N/A	Car and Driver
1972 911S	2.4-liter	6.0	14.4	N/A	Car and Driver
1973 Carrera RSR	2.7-liter	5.6	13.2	N/A	Road & Track
1974 911	2.7-liter	7.9	15.5	130	Road & Track
1975 Calif. Carrera	2.7-liter	8.2	16.5	134	Road & Track
1975 Turbo	3.0-liter	5.5[2]	24.21[1]	152.9	Automobil Revue (Swiss)
1976 935 Turbo	2.8-liter	3.3	8.9	150	Road & Track
1978 911SC	3.0-liter	6.3	15.3	N/A	Road & Track
1979 930 Turbo	3.3-liter	5.3	13.4	160	Motor
1980 911SC	3.0-liter	7.0	N/A	141	Porsche
1984 Carrera	3.2-liter	5.6	N/A	159	Autocar
1990 Carrera 2	3.6-liter	5.7	N/A	162	Porsche
1990 Carrera Tiptronic	3.6-liter	6.2	N/A	157	Porsche
1991 Turbo	3.3-liter	5.0[2]	N/A	168	Porsche
1993 RS America	3.6-liter	5.4	N/A	162	Porsche
1995 Turbo	3.6-liter	3.9	12.5	180	Road & Track
1998 993	3.6-liter	5.4	N/A	171	Porsche
1999 996	3.4-liter	5.2	N/A	174	Porsche

[1] One kilometer distance from standing start.
[2] 0 to 62 miles per hour (100 kilometers per hour)

NOTE: Information for this chart has been compiled from various sources and does not necessarily represent the definitive performance of any of the models listed. Its purpose is to entertain 911 aficionados as much as enlighten them.

BIBLIOGRAPHY

Adler, Dennis. *Porsche 911 Road Cars*. Osceola, Wisconsin: MBI Publishing Company, 1998.

Aichele, Tobias. *Porsche 911, Forever Young*. Stuttgart, Germany: Motorbuch-Verlag, 1993.

Anderson, Bruce. *Porsche 911 Performance Handbook*. Osceola, Wisconsin: MBI Publishing Company, 1996.

Boschen, Lothar and Jurgen Barth. *The Porsche Book*. New York City: Arco Publishing, Inc., 1977.

Flammang, James M. *Standard Catalog of Imported Cars 1946–1990*. Iola, Wisconsin: Krause Publications, Inc., 1994.

Frere, Paul. *Porsche 911 Story*, 6th edition. Somerset, England: Patrick Stephens, Limited, 1997.

Harvey, Chris. *The Porsche 911*. Somerset, England: The Oxford Illustrated Press, 1983.

James, Drayton, Editor. *The Porsche Family Tree*. Vienna, VA: Porsche Club of America, PEA, Porsche Club of America, 1995.

Leffingwell, Randy. *Legendary Porsche*. Osceola, Wisconsin: MBI Publishing Company, 1996.

Ludvigsen, Karl. *Porsche, Excellence Was Expected*. Princeton, NJ: Princeton Publishing, Inc., 1977.

Morgan, Peter. *Original Porsche 911*. Osceola, Wisconsin: MBI Publishing Company, 1998.

Starkey, John. *Porsche 911 R-RS-RSR*. Dorchester, England: Veloce Publishing Plc., 1998.

CLUBS AND SOURCES FOR THE PORSCHE 911

The Early 911S Registry
P.O. Box 16001
Newport Beach, CA   92659-6001
www.911sregistry.org
Fax 949-642-9543

R Gruppe (early 911 performance and vintage race cars)
Cris Huergas
1530 Court Street
Alameda, CA   94501
e-mail: crispin_d_huergas@ffic.com

Porsche Owners Club
Hotline: 310-784-5653
www.porscheclub.com

PML, The Market Letter for Porsche Automobiles
P.O. Box 6010
Oceanside, CA   92058
888-928-9111
www.pmletter.com
e-mail: pmletter@aol.com

Porsche Club of America
PCA National Office
P.O. Box 30100
Alexandria, VA 22310
703-922-9300
www.pca.org

INDEX